Recipes

of

Old England

T0386663

Recipes

of

Old England

Three Centuries of
English Cooking: 1580–1850

modernised by

Bernard N. Bessunger

David & Charles : Newton Abbot

Set in 11 on 13pt Caslon
and printed in Great Britain
by Latimer Trend & Company Ltd Plymouth
for David & Charles (Holdings) Limited
South Devon House Newton Abbot Devon

Contents

List of Illustrations

8

"Sir", said Dr Johnson, after examining a French Menu, "my brain is obfuscated after the perusal of this heterogeneous conglomeration of bastard English ill-spelt, and a foreign tongue. I prithee bid thy knaves bring a dish of hog's puddings, a slice or two from the upper cut of a well roasted sirloin, and two apple-dumplings."

Preface

"It being grown as unfashionable for a Book now to appear in Public without a Preface, as for a Lady to appear at a Ball without a Hoop-Petticoat; I shall conform to Custom for Fashion sake, and not through any Necessity: The Subject being both common and universal, needs no Arguments to introduce it, and being so necessary for the Gratification of the Appetite, stands in need of no Encomium to allure Persons to the Practice of it, since there are but few now-a-days who love not Good Eating and Drinking; therefore I entirely quit those two Topics; but having three or four pages to be filled up previous to the Subject itself, I shall employ them on a Subject I think new, and yet not handled by any of the Pretenders to the Art of Cookery; and that is the Antiquity of it; which, if it either instruct or divert, I shall be satisfied if you are so."

The Compleat Housewife or Accomplish'd Gentlewoman's Companion, 15th edition, 1753. By Eliza Smith.

Foreword

In this brief collation of old English recipes I have purposely chosen the period under review because, while the reign of Elizabeth I was a period of intense nationalism, yet by then the Renaissance, with all that it implied, was flourishing throughout the Europe of which the English were so much a part. Spreading from Italy, the new march of intellect seemed to make each country address its peculiar genius to the table and the pursuit of good living. The somewhat barbarous approach to food which characterised the Middle Ages, when culinary prowess was achieved more by quantity than quality, and the composition of feasts given by the Courts and noblemen of the great European houses read like a gorgeous farrago of indigestibility. They can be deciphered more for amusement than instruction, and the groaning board was no idle figure of speech. . .

The records are there, of course, of countless dishes devised by master cooks in the preceding centuries, but I would scarcely weary the reader with putative adaptations of such delights as *Fesaunt intramde Royall, Swan with Chawdron, Crane with Cretney, Heronusen with his Sique, Rabett Sowker, Larkes ingrayled, Pekoke in Hakell* and *Egrets in Beorwetye*, to be eaten with the fingers aided by small sidearms. This is the stuff of antiquarian research, but not, I felt, within the scope of the practical book I hoped to write.

Here, rather, is an attempt to distil the essence of those old days when cooks knew no 'convenience' foods, no frosted peas, no fish fingers or frozen beef-burgers; but old days in which our English cooks and housewives exercised their native ingenuity to provide the table with a variety of good fare, much of which in the last hundred years has been forgotten. For it is the technicological 'advances' of that period which have at last brought us to the edge of the descent to that culinary Avernus where, all ready for us, are meat analogues of synthetically flavoured spun-protein which at will may become 'beef', 'veal', 'chicken' or 'ham'. Doubtless there are sound sociological reasons for all this, and an overpopulated world will feel obliged to the scientists who made it possible.

But while there is still a chance, perhaps some of us may care to throw a backward glance without any sentimental nostalgia, and try for themselves what they have missed. In collecting material I have had to discard much that is not really practical because of our differing life-style, and because many of the published works in past centuries were intended for a readership of large households.

What emerged quite strongly from reading these bygone kitchen exercises was that, apart from the unsuspectedly wide range of ingredients, there were a great many simple dishes. It is easy to form the impression that the English were a nation of mighty trenchermen, consistently stuffing themselves at table and meeting an early death from chronic dyspepsia and liver complaints. But those staggering old menus so often quoted as typical, frequently meant that a wide choice was given to the guests, and then only on an 'occasion'. In extracting the simpler and more practical dishes I have used, in roughly equal proportion, both old printed and manuscript sources. I hope the reader will share with me the peculiar charm of the latter, in which the personality of the writers seems to emerge almost as if one had actual contact with them, standing by their great open fires watching the spits revolve, or gossiping over tea and cakes with their neighbours.

I have been further encouraged by what seems today a notable revival of interest in authentically *English* cooking and perhaps some small animadversion toward the continental and oriental which have filled our cookery book shelves for so long. Not that I share the rabid xenophobia which afflicted the old writers in their own prefatory remarks, one or two examples of which I have given; but now that we are all officially Europeans perhaps our neighbours should be given an opportunity to sample our own indigenous cooking rather than the pale travesties of theirs.

In opting for 1850 as the terminal year of 'old' English cookery, I felt that the more general use of gas for domestic purposes initiated a revolution in cooking which presaged the age in which we live and eat today; in a few years Mrs Beeton was to write her deathless *Household Management*, the new railways had speeded communications with an impact comparable only to the aeroplane, the old coaching inns were dying of inanition, the manufacture of canned meats had begun, and the dear Queen had established by her marriage continental connections which were reflected in the kitchens of her loyal people; it became modish to call almost everything *à la* this and that, puddings became 'Coburg', 'Nesselrode' or even just 'German', and even apple charlotte became *Charlotte de pomme*. Restaurant English was upon us, and a new era had dawned in the kitchen. Which, I wonder, was the better?

The frequent call for 'orange flower water' and 'rose water' in the old kitchen need not daunt the experimental cook. While at one time they were the ordinary stock-in-trade of the grocer, they can be made up on demand by any good pharmaceutical chemist (but avoid the cosmetic counter where they are compounded in facial lotions!). Alternatively try a herbalist, or omit them entirely.

Appliances and Methods

A short summary of the methods of the old cooks and their culinary equipment may assist the reader to understand the instructions in many of the old receipts given. If they can form a mental picture, however hazy, of the cook at work in the period under review, then they may care to make adaptations which may well vary from mine and come closer to the originals.

What becomes apparent on examining the general *batterie de cuisine* of two or three hundred years ago, is the marked similarity to our own. Allowing for the absence of modern kitchen 'gadgets', refrigerators, electrically driven mixers and other 'labour-saving' devices, who could not set up house with the following list? Compiled in a book published in the seventeenth century entitled *A Perfect School of Instruction for the Officers of the Mouth*, by Giles Rose, a former cook to the king, it runs:

> "First a copper oven, 3 skillets [heavy iron pot or stew-pan], an Iron Furnace, a preserving Pan, a Fish Pan, a stone Mortar with a Pestle, a Nest of 6 Pots one in another, sausepans twelve, small Gembole [ie twin, Ed.] Racks with Broatches [spits], small and great larding Pins, ladles, scummer, cullenders, a Chopping Knife, a Mincing Knife and many such like not inserted here."

It is important to remember that all *roasting* and *grilling* was done before an open fire (there being no 'public services' for heating food!) and *baking* in an oven, so that only those with an electric spit can today hope to follow receipts for roasts very exactly. Wood was the principal fuel, with charcoal added to give an intense, smokeless heat, what they called 'sea-coal' being reserved for industrial uses (such as smelting and glass-blowing), and, later, domestic heating. Spit-cooking was universal, from the primitive wrought-iron rod, resting on 'dogs' at either side of the fire and turned by hand, to mechanically driven elaborations of the same principle, powered by clockwork motors, or wretched hounds and other devices. Most households would have a collection of spits, heavy for meat, fine for poultry, and one with a metal cage for cooking fish whole. Other methods of roasting involved the use of a bottle-jack, which hung vertically from an adjustable crane-hook before the fire and turned slowly by clockwork. (These latter were commonly used in the country and made right up to the 1930s, when I bought the one illustrated from a large department-store's stock in London.) Hot water was normally supplied from a large iron pot suspended over or placed on the fire, in which could also be immersed a smaller, earthenware vessel to achieve the type of cooking we term 'jugging', eg hare, and for boiling puddings in their cloths. The copper oven to which Rose refers was what even today survives in old houses as the 'copper', used for heating water and boiling washing. Larger households were often equipped with a type of stove on which pots could be placed for keeping food warm, or *bain-marie* cooking (see illustration p 87), a replica of which can be seen today in many hotel kitchens. *Baking* of pies etc was largely done in a brick oven at the side of the fire opening, the primary use of which was baking the household loaves, and was fired with brushwood and charcoal or logs to intense heat, the ashes being then swept out, and the dough put in. It retained its heat sufficiently after the bread was 'enough' to cook the pies and pastries required.

The use of the preserving pan, of course, was not restricted to today's annual orgy of jam-making and fruit-bottling, but in general use for potting meats, pickles, store sauces, confectionery and in fact the things for which we now go to the grocer's or the supermarket. The households in all classes of society were of necessity much more self-contained, and work in the kitchen, even in the towns, meant ceaseless activity for the housewife and her servants. For those who were not inclined to cook, roast joints, fowls and pies could be obtained from the cook shop—an activity now reflected in the modern addiction to 'take-aways'. There was considerable public outcry when these facilities were withdrawn on Sundays during the Commonwealth.

With the advent of food technology, the kitchen has shrunk in size but not, as some would have it, in importance, and those who are not entirely content with 'convenience foods', may still simulate the old cooks, with the advantage of less labour. This is not to say that ingenious minds were not at work in the old days. The antiquarian Anthony à Wood, in his notes for November 1698, quotes a handbill, or what we might call a press-release, for a kind of super-spit, fully automatic:

"Money well bestow'd. At the Chequer Inn in *Oxford* will be shown diverss Rarities, performed upon SPITS: the first and all that was ever made in *England* . . .
First, It Roasts Six or Seven Sorts or Dishes of Meat by a Fire Eighteen Inches long, all Joynts distinct from each other, not one Dripping upon another: It Basts the Meat, without any Persons attendance: and Roasts quicker and much cleaner than any other way; the Spits from Morning to Night go alone, without Jacks, lines, Weights, Strings or Pullies.
Secondly, It Frys Fish and Felsh with a great deal of Curiosity, turning all the Fish . . .
Thirdly, It Broils and Roasts any sort of Meat, Apples, or Eggs.
Fourthly, It Bakes Custards, Cheese-cakes, Puddings,

19

Tarts and Pyes, extreamely sweet and clean.

Fiftly, It Stews and Boyles a good Joynt of Meat with Roots and Herbs, and you may eat a good mess of Broth boyled upon the Spit; the Spits always going alone."

Unfortunately no single example of this masterly labour-saver seems to have survived. Or perhaps like so many inventors, he was bought out by contemporary vested interests—the standard spit manufacturers . . .

Another remarkable innovation came on the market at about the same time, the original pressure cooker. This was the brain-child of Dr Denis Papin FRS, whose somewhat unwieldy machine is illustrated on p 34. The use of this is again recorded by another learned diarist, John Evelyn, on 12 April 1682:

"I went this Afternoon to a Supper, with severall of the R. Society, which was all dressed (both fish and flesh) in *M. Papin's Digestorie*, by which the hardest bones of Biefe . . . were without water or other liquor . . . made as soft as Cheeze . . . & for close, a Gellie, the most delicious I have ever seene or tasted . . . but nothing exceeded the Pigeons, which tasted just as if baked in a pie . . ."

According to Dr Kitchiner in *The Cook's Oracle* a modified and improved version of a Cast Iron Digester was for sale 'at *Jackson and Moser's*, in Frith Street Soho', in 1817. Today, old Papin's idea of an autoclave cooker has a place on most kitchen shelves.

And now that we are seeing a revival of the art and mystery of spit-cooking in electrical form, a final word to the initiates. It was roasting in the old manner which gave real meaning to the words of the triumphant cook—*done to a turn!*

Soups

SOUP MEAGRE

"Take four large Cucumbers cut into Slices ditto Onions
—four Lettuces cut into quarters and ¼lb Butter put them
all into a stewpan and stew them over the fire till they are
tender—take three pints of old Pease and let them boil in
four quarts of water and a bunch of Mint when they are
soft pass them through a Seive—Season the Soup with a
little Pepper and Salt adding the Stewed Vegetables and
serve it up—Miss A. Penkett (1800)"

*Amy Hull Family MS Receipt Book (see page 22). Loaned by
Miss Hull.*

———————————

Another similar MS recipe (1811) suggests 'an anchovy or two
instead of salt'. There are endless versions of *soup maigre* in old
cookery books based on whatever flavour you wished to predominate,
eg onion, carrot, chestnut, etc. I selected this MS version because of
the unusual cucumber base. Since one is hardly likely to require a
gallon of soup for a small dinner, I cut down the vegetable quantities
(2 cucumbers, peeled, 1 onion, 2 lettuces), and cheated the time-
consuming process of boiling dried peas by substituting 2 cans of Pea

Soup, suitably diluted with milk, added the mint, and served with a spoonful of cream on each plate with a little chopped parsley. It was approved.

This, and further receipts under this name are derived from an old family MS collection of which the owner writes:

'I had this book from my mother, and she was born in 1857. She told me that many of the receipts were originally given by my great-grandfather's gardener, Sam Bell, and others by my mother's older cousin, H. J. Crump.'

From this we can fairly assume that they belong to the mid-eighteenth century, and would be typical of country-house fare of that period.

SPRING SOUP

> "Take twelve lettuces, cut them in slices and put them into strong Broth, get six green cucumbers, pare them, and cut out the Cores, cut them into little Bits, and scald them in boiling Water, and put them into your Broth, let them boil very tender with a mutchkin of young Pease and some Crumbs of Bread."

A New and Easy Method of Cookery. Chiefly Intended for the Benefit of the Young Ladies who Attend Her School. By Elizabeth Cleland, 1759.

This is a meatier version of Soup Meagre. Take as much good stock as you require, 5 lettuces (the small, early variety) and 2 large cucumbers—the author probably used the variety we call 'ridge'—and enough young peas, when shelled, to measure ½ pint. Peel the cucumbers, dice them, sprinkle well with salt and allow to drain. Simmer them with the lettuce in the well-seasoned stock. If you like it thick add the bread-crumbs. I served it simply with fried *croûtons*.

SALLY'S WHITE SOUP—SWANSEA

"Stew a Knuckle of veal with onions turnips & a little mace for three or four hours then strain it & let it stand skimming off all the fat—when you want to use it—thicken it with a little flour & milk—boil it up with some Macaroni —have ready mixed in the tureen the yolks of one or two eggs well beat & a wine glass of white wine—& pour the boiling soup to it gently stirring it all the time—that it may not curdle."

MS Receipt Book, Catherine Dixon, circa 1811. *Loaned by Miss M. Aldred, FRSA.*

A whole knuckle of veal will be too much for the average household, so you can either buy (or beg) some soup bones from the butcher, or, as I did, substitute 2 or 3 cans of beef consommé. In this cook 1 onion and a couple of turnips chopped up. Season well and cook these until tender (not 4 hours) and the flavour extracted. Strain and thicken as directed, and put in a handful of vermicelli well broken, when it comes to boil. While this is cooking, beat up the egg-yolks and dry white wine in the tureen, and follow the rest of the direction.

The owner writes:

"This (MS) book was put together by the daughters of Admiral Dixon over a period from 1811 to 1853. Their father was the son of Admiral Sir Manley Dixon, whose distinguished naval career included the capture of the Island of Malta from the French in the Napoleonic Wars."

It will thus be seen that these receipts are typical of those used in an upper middle-class household at the beginning of the last century.

GOURD, OR VEGETABLE MARROW, SOUP

"Should be made of full-grown Gourds, but not those that have hard skins; slice three or four, and put them in a stew-pan, with two or three Onions, and a good bit of Butter; set them over a slow fire till quite tender (be careful not to let them burn) then add two ounces of crust of Bread, and two quarts of good *Consommé*; season with salt and Cayenne pepper: boil ten minutes, or a quarter of an hour; skim off all the fat, and pass it through a tamis; then make it quite hot, and serve up with fried bread."

(This is accompanied by the following letter.)

"The following Receipts are from Mr HENRY OSBORNE, Cook to SIR JOSEPH BANKS, the late President of the Royal Society:

Soho Square, April 20, 1820

SIR—I send you herewith the last part of the *Cook's Oracle*. I have attentively looked over each receipt, and hope they are now correct, and easy to be understood. If you think any need further explanation, Sir Joseph has desired me to wait on you again. I also send the Receipts for my ten Puddings, and my method of using Spring Fruit and Gourds.

I am, SIR,

Your humble Servant,

HENRY OSBORNE."

Apicius Redevivus or The Cook's Oracle. By William Kitchiner, MD, 1817.

The author was a wealthy physician and *bon viveur* who did not practise his profession, but preferred to advise the public of his (sometimes bizarre) general views on diet and cookery through his books, which were extremely popular. *The Cook's Oracle* went through eleven editions between 1817 and 1840, and an abbreviated version was published as late as 1861 under the title *The Shilling Kitchiner*. He declared in his introduction that '. . . the Author has submitted to a labour no preceding Cookery Book maker ever attempted to encounter—having *eaten* each Receipt before he set it down in his book'. He was extremely popular among a wide circle of friends, many of whom were artists and musicians, and possibly this remark was a result of his weekly dinner parties at his house in Bloomsbury given to a select circle whom he designated as *The Committee of Taste*. He further has the distinction of being occasionally plagiarised by Brillat-Savarin, writing ten years later and evidently familiar with his work. The above receipt from the edition of 1821 I have selected (from the list appended to Mr Osborne's letter) as being of more special interest than the remainder, dealing as it does with the problem of rendering the somewhat vapid vegetable marrow into a palatable soup. As an alternative to the onions I have used tomato with a hint of garlic on occasion.

TURNIP SOUP

"1 Doz turnips, 6 onions, 2 heads of Celery sliced thin, a small piece of lean Bacon, a few white pepper corns, the crumb of a french Roll, put these into 3 quarts of Water, or broth, boil them gently till quite soft, skim it and bruise the turnips, then put it all thro' a Sieve, have ready boiled in water some turnips cut in dice add a pint of cream, a little salt (mace if you please) the top of a small loaf or french roll, let it boil up once altogether."

MS Receipt Book, Catherine Dixon, circa 1811. *Loaned by Miss Aldred, Devon.*

Adjust the quantities to need, eg for four servings 6 medium turnips, 3 onions, a head of celery, a heaped tablespoon of breadcrumbs, 3 pints of water or stock (diluted canned *consommé* or beefstock cubes will serve). Follow the writer's instructions and put all through the blender. Add the prepared, diced turnip, season, and thicken with a small carton of cream. Heat up, serve with fried *croûtons* and a spoonful of cream in each serving. *It is as well to remember, when reading these old receipts that in this, as in many others, a pint was sixteen fluid ounces, compared with today's twenty, which may modify the alarm felt at first sight.*

Egg Dishes

PORTUGUEZ EGGS

"The way that the Countess de Penalva makes the Portu-
guez Eggs for the Queen, is this. Take the yolks (clean
picked from the whites and germ) of twelve new-laid
Eggs. Beat them exceedingly with a little (scarce a spoonful) of Orange-flower-water. When they are exceeding
liquid, clear, and uniformly a thin Liquor, put to them
one pound of pure double refined Sugar (if it be not so
pure, it must be clarified before) and stew them in your
dish or bason over a very gentle fire, stirring them continually, whiles they are over it, so that the whole may
become one uniform substance, of the consistence of an
Electuary (beware they grow not too hard; for without
much caution and attention, that will happen on a sudden)
which then you may eat presently, or put into pots to keep.
You may dissolve Ambergreece (if you will, ground first
very much with Sugar) in Orange-flower or Rose-water,
before hand, and put it (warm and dissolved) to the Eggs,
when you set them to stew. If you clarifie your Sugar, do
it with one of these waters, and whites of Eggs. The flavor
of these sweet-waters goeth almost all away with boiling.
Therefore half a spoonful put into the composition, when

you take it from the fire, seasoneth it more then ten times as much, put in at the first."

The Closet of the Eminently Learned Sir Kenelm Digby, Kt, Opened 1669.

The Queen referred to was Henrietta Maria, wife of Charles I (see Biographical Notes), by whom Digby was sent to Rome to raise money for the Stuart cause in the role of Ambassador.

The 'Electuary' to which he refers was a common term at that time for any medicinal powder dissolved in honey or syrup. His warning is best observed by making this in a double-boiler, like *hollandaise* sauce. Use the number of eggs you require, keeping the proportion of eggs to sugar (icing sugar is best). Short of the required orange-flower water, use a little almond or vanilla essence, or if you are so disposed, a spoonful of rum or even madeira, with which the countess of Penalva was probably acquainted.

A FRICASEE OF EGGS

"Boil six eggs hard, slice them in round slices, then stew some morels in white wine, with an eschalot, two anchovies, a little thyme, a few oysters or cockles, and salt, to your taste; when they have stew'd well together, put in your eggs and a bit of butter; toss them up together till it is thick, and then serve it up."

The Compleat Housewife or Accomplish'd Gentlewoman's Companion, *15th edition,* 1753. *By Eliza Smith.*

As 'morels' are obtainable commercially only in France (*Les*

28

Morilles! Ce nom seul fait venir l'eau à la bouche. O. Foucher: 'Bons et Mauvais Champignons'), we must perforce use mushrooms, and preferably 'flaps', not the buttons, which are decorative but tasteless.

Substitute canned baby clams, now pretty generally obtainable, for the oysters or cockles, and you have an unusual Sunday breakfast or supper.

AN EGG CHEESE

"Take three mutchkins (three pints) of sweet cream or good milk; put it on with a little cinnamon, lemon-peel, sugar and half a mutchkin (half a pint) of white wine; cast a dozen of eggs; keeping out six of the whites; mix the eggs very well with the cold milk; put it on the fire, and keep it stirring all the time until it comes a boil. When you see it is broke, turn it out into any shape you have, with holes; let it stand until the whey runs from it, and turn it out of the shape. You may flavour it either with orange-flower or rose-water before you put it into the shape. If you choose, you may pour sweet cream over it, or it may be eat with wine and sugar."

The Practice of Cookery, Pastry, Confectionary, Pickling, Preserving etc, 1795. *By Mrs Frazer.*

———————————

This appears to be a refined, or table, version of a posset (which latter was generally reserved for winter colds or the megrims). I reduced the quantities to 1 pint Jersey milk, 4 eggs, 1 glass of sweet white wine, and put the mixture in a colander over a basin, and served it chilled.

TO FRICASSEE EGGS BROWN

"Boil as many eggs hard as you want to fill your dish: take off the shells and fry them in butter, of a fine brown; pour your fat out of the pan, put in some flour and a lump of butter, stir it till it is thick and of a good brown; pour in some boiling water, a gill of Madeira, a little pepper, salt and beaten mace: boil all together till it is of a good thickness; scum it, and squeeze in a little orange; cut some of your eggs in half, lay the flat side uppermost, and the whole ones between; pour the sauce over. Garnish with fried parsley and a Sevill orange cut in quarters."

The Frugal Housewife, or Complete Woman Cook by Susannah Carter of Clerkenwell, London 1795.

The original publication seems, as was not unusual, to have been pirated some years later, and then appeared as: 'Originally written by Susanna Carter: but now improved by an experienced cook in one of the principal Taverns in the City of London, 1823.'

———————

This bears all the attributes of a Regency gentleman's breakfast, probably preceded by mutton chops and a pint of claret, having ridden to the City from Hampstead or Islington. In our less vigorous society it makes an excellent supper, and the combination of eggs, Madeira and orange well worth the experiment.

TO DRESS EGGS CALLED IN FRENCH
A la Augenotte, or the Protestant way

"Break twenty eggs beat them together and put to them pure Gravy of a leg of Mutton or the Gravy of roast Beef, stir and beat them well together over a Chaffindish, with a little salt. Add to them also Juice of Orange and Lemon or grape verjuice; then put in some Mushrooms well boyled and seasoned. Observe, as soon as your eggs be well mixed with the Gravy and other Ingredients, then take off the fire, keeping them covered awhile. Then serve them with grated Nutmeg over them."

The Whole Body of Cookery Dissected. By William Rabisha, London 1673. Master Cook to many honourable Families before and since the wars began, both in this my Native Countrey, and with Embassadors and other Nobles in certain forraign parts.

This receipt resolves itself best as a sort of enriched scrambled egg, or *oeufs brouillés*, if made with 3 or 4 eggs. Beat them up well in the ordinary way, adding a little good stock and a few drops of wine vinegar or lemon juice, but not so much as to make your mixture too liquid. Prepare some sliced mushrooms gently fried in butter with milled pepper and salt. Put a good lump of butter in a saucepan, pour in the egg mixture and stir well, adding the mushrooms when it starts to cook. By 'take off the fire' Master Rabisha would have meant reduce the cooking heat in modern terms, as he would have used an open fire under his chafing-dish. Once again the inevitable nutmeg appears, but to my mind it is an optional extra. His book was popular at the time and was reprinted in successive editions, one of which contains a frightful recipe 'To roast a shoulder of Mutton in Blood'!

Fish

"Of all nacyone and countres, England is best serued of Fysshe, not only of all manner of see-fysshe, but also of fresshe-water fysshe, and all manner of sortes of salte-fysshe."

Andrew Boorde's *Dyetary of Helthe* 1542

A NOTE ON FISH

Fish has always been an important item in the traditional English kitchen, since apart from the length of coast line and the numbers engaged in extracting a livelihood from the surrounding seas, the edicts of the medieval church left an indelible imprint on the diet of succeeding centuries. Their old 'fysshe days' were not restricted to Fridays and Lent, and thus considerable ingenuity of preparation finds a place in all old cookery books.

Transport from the coasts, however, due to the state, and often the absence, of roads, necessitated pickling, smoking and preserving of all save freshwater fish, and thus frequent references to oysters, stockfish, herring, cod and many others would have applied principally to those barrelled or salted and dried. The frequent mention of oysters for stuffings, sauces etc may appear strange to us, but this now costly commodity was so common it was sold from stalls in the streets and was even fed to his cat by Dr Johnson! That today some of these methods linger in our present day fare with herring, haddock, cod, cod-roe,

Page 33 'The Hoop and Grapes' in Aldgate was the last tavern in London to use the roasting spit until a few years ago, when it was demolished. Note the spit and pot-crane for hanging a bottle-jack

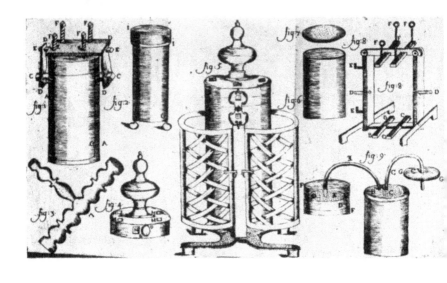

Page 34   (top) *Dr Denys Papin's Digestorie* (*the first pressure-cooker*), 1681; (below) *clockwork bottle-jack adjustable for height*

mackerel etc, is largely because of the ingenuity of the methods of early fish merchants in not only preserving but giving their material additional zest. The appearance of the *anchovy* in many of these old receipts is worth attention, since its use as an alternate for salt in all manner of sauces, pies etc produces a fine flavour, in combination, which can hardly be achieved with anything else. Those who would endeavour to match their skill with that of the old cooks should have this little fish always available.

Robert Burton, in his dietary examinations in the *Anatomy of Melancholy* (1621), writes: 'Gomesius doth immoderately extol sea-fish and above the rest dried, soused, indurate fish, as ling, fumados, red-herrings, sprats, stockfish, haberdine, poor-john, all shell-fish.' It was the country folk and the dedicated anglers who from necessity, and possibly preference, were obliged to rely on freshwater fish, and the well stocked and unpolluted rivers remained an excellent source of supply. The landed gentry and yeoman farmers generally maintained their own fish ponds—a legacy from the old monastic houses—from which they could cull a plentiful supply at will of eel, carp, tench, trout and even pike. For the reader whose tastes are in that direction I can recommend no better source of culinary information than old Izaak Walton's *Compleat Angler* (1653), where his occasional notes on 'dressing' his catch have perhaps more validity than his charming advice on fishing for it. His method of spit-roasting pike, stuffed with herbs, anchovy and garlic butter should prove an interesting exercise in adapting the seventeenth to the twentieth century.

TO MAKE A CRABSCOE OF CRAWFISH

"Take about a Quarter of an Hundred or more of Craw-fish, take out the tails then pound the shells very fine, then put them in a stewpan with about a Pound of good butter, set it over a gentle Fire and let it stew a good while, then strain the Butter into another Stewpan and let it stand to

be cold, then work it to a Cream with a wooden Ladle or
Spoon, then by Degrees add to it yolks of Eggs, the crumb
of a french Roll steep'd in Cream, a little Lemon Peel and
Nutmeg, if you have it sweet add a little Sugar and work it
all together well with a little Cream, then make a Rim of
Paste round the Dish put in your Ingredients, stick the
tails of your Crawfish in it and so bake it—half an Hour
bakes it."

Dorset Dishes of the 17th *Century, collected by J. Stevens Cox, FSA,*
1967. *MS recipe from the Bragge family of Beaminster and Sadborrow*

This splendidly titled dish seems an example of the unfortunate
confusion of *crawfish* with *crayfish*, which persists even today; so let us
clearly establish that the Bragge family's crawfish were evidently the
small river crayfish (Fr: *écrevisse*) so abundant in Sweden that the first
of August, the opening of the *Kräftor* season, is almost a national
holiday. It is recorded that the daily consumption in Stockholm alone
is in the region of 1½ million, and traditionally the breaking of each
claw is accompanied by a glass of Schnapps . . . Here, alas! they are
rarely seen and difficult to find. In modern culinary terms crawfish is
the spiny, or 'rock' lobster (Fr: *langouste*), a much longer beast.

To effect a compromise I substituted Dublin Bay prawns, which can
be bought in the shell, and employed the following method:

Take two dozen prawns (or 'scampi'), shell them, but leave on the
head and claws; pound the shells in a mortar, brown them in butter as
in the original receipt (I used ½lb), then add sufficient water just to
cover. Boil up, and allow to simmer for a good 15 minutes, strain into
another saucepan and remove to a cool place. When the butter on top
has hardened, drain and beat up as specified, add the yolks of 2 eggs
gradually. Meanwhile have by you 4 heaped tablespoons of breadcrumbs soaked in milk and squeezed out (panada)—cream will make it
too rich and at that time was often synonymous with unskimmed milk

—to which you have added a teaspoon of grated lemon-peel, nutmeg, and a sprinkle of paprika just to colour it. (I did not 'have it sweet' and can scarcely recommend this variation.) Mix all well together and put in the centre of your flat buttered baking-dish. Surround the rim with a border of your favourite pastry, well glazed with egg, and stick the prawns in it, head outwards, round the dish. Bake as required.

BECHEMELE OF FISH

"Pike, Cod or Skate pick them from the bones. To one pound of this add ½ pint cream 1½ spoonful of Anchovy liquor or Essence 1 teaspoonful good mustard, 1 do Catsup, pepper to your taste. When nearly hot add a little flour and butter—make it quite hot and put it in a dish then strow bread crumbs over it—baste it with butter till the crumbs are quite moist—then salamander it."

Manuscript cookery book: Mrs F. Briggs, Wigmore Street, 1825. Blanche Leigh Collection, Brotherton Library, University of Leeds, MS 60.

Any firm white fish will serve for this variation on the familiar and somewhat boring fish in white sauce, served in scallop shells, piped round with mashed potato. The difference here lies in first heating up the fish in your saucepan with the flavourings as given. (Cream and milk in equal proportion will make it less rich.) For the 'Catsup' substitute either bottled mushroom or tomato ketchup. After thickening, it looks better put into individual ramekins, before bread-crumbing and finishing under the hot grill as instructed.

TO DRESSE FLOUNDERS OR PLAYCE
WITH GARLICK AND MUSTARD

"Take Flounders very new, and cut all the Fins and
Tailes, then take out the Guts and wipe them very clean,
they must not be all washt, then with your Knife Scotch
them on both sides very grosely; then take the Tops of
Tyme and cut them very small, and take a little Salt,
Mace, and Nutmeg, and mingle the Tyme and them together, and season the Flounders; then lay them on the
Gridiron and bast them with Oyle or Butter, let not the
fire be too hot, when that side next the fire is brown, turn it,
and when you turn it, bast it on both sides till you have
broyl'd them brown; when they are enough make your
sauce with Mustard two or three spoonfull according to
discretion, six Anchovies dissolved very well, about halfe
a pound of butter drawn up with garlick, vinegar, or
bruised garlick in other vinegar, rubb the bottome of your
Dish with garlick. So put your sauce to them and serve
them."

*The Compleat Cook. Expertly prescribing the most ready wayes for
dressing of Flesh, and Fish, ordering of Sauces or Making of Pastry.
London. Printed by E.B. for Nath. Brook at the Angel in Cornhill,
1658.*

In this instance, *c'est la sauce qui fait le poisson*, as the French insist.
You will hardly need ½lb of butter, and the mustard should be of the
bland French variety. Go steady on the garlic, or you won't taste the
fish!

OYSTER LOAVES

"Make a round hole at the tops of some little round loaves,
and scrape out the crumb. Put some oysters into a tossing-
pan* with the oyster liquor, and the crumbs that were
taken out of the loaves, and a large piece of butter. Stew
them together for five or six minutes; then put in a
spoonful of good cream, and fill your loaves. Then lay the
bit of crust carefully on the top again, and put them in the
oven to crisp."

*The London Art of Cookery, and Housekeeper's Complete Assistant. On
a New Plan. Made Plain and Easy to the Understanding of every
Housekeeper, Cook, and Servant in the Kingdom. By John Farley,
Principal Cook at the London Tavern. Original edition* 1783, *reprinted*
12 *times, last edition* 1811.

I tried this with mussels cooked in a little white wine, using large
bread-rolls. For a quick and pain-free first course, try those canned
American oysters, heated in their own juice. Wipe the rolls with a
damp cloth before heating, to prevent a charcoal finish!

A PHRAISE OF COCKLES

"Take your Cockles, boyl them and pick them out of the
shells, wash them clean from gravel, then break a dozen
eggs with a little Nutmeg, Cinamon and Ginger, and put
your Cockles therein, and beat them together with a
handful of grated bread, a quarter of a pint of cream, then
put Butter in to your Frying-pan, and let it be hot, as for

* Frying-pan.

39

eggs, and put in the Phraise: supply it with Butter in the sides of the pan, and let the thin of the eggs run stiff into the middle, till it moves round; and when it is fryed on that side, butter your plate and turn it and put it into your Pan again and fry the other side brown; then take it forth and dish it, and scruise on the juice of Lemmons, and strow on Ginger and Cinamon, and send it up; you may green it with Spinnage, and cut it out into quarters, and garnish your fish, or either sort; thus may you fry Pranes, Perriwinkles or other shell fish."

The Whole Body of Cookery Dissected by William Rabisha, London **1673**. *Master Cook to many honourable Families before and since the wars began, both in this my Native Countrey, and with Embassadors and other Nobles in certain forraign parts*

This 'phraise' or fraze as it was more usually spelt, the reader will recognise as a sort of omelette of the kind we now term 'Spanish' The cockles are more easily obtained today in a jar or tin, unless you acquire them from the fishmonger or the cockle-stall, still happily with us. Obviously you will use the number of eggs you require, spice them very lightly and follow the author's directions. You may prefer to garnish the dish with lemon quarters or slices and omit further ginger and cinnamon. As he says, it is good served on its own, or as a side plate for a main fish course. 'Pranes', of course, are prawns.

TO PICKLE MUSCLES OR COCKLES

"Take your fresh muscles or cockles, wash them very clean, and put them in a pot over the fire till they open; then take them out of their shells, pick them clean, and lay

them to cool; then put their liquor to some vinegar, whole
pepper, ginger sliced thin, and mace, setting it over the
fire; when 'tis scalding hot put in your muscles, and let
them stew a little; then pour out the pickle from them,
and when both are cold put them in an earthen jug, and
cork it up close: in two or three days they will be fit to
eat."

*The London Cook, or the Whole Art of Cookery Made Easy and Fami-
liar, by William Gelleroy, Late Cook to her Grace the Dutchess of
Argyle. And now to the Right Hon Sir Samuel Fludyer Bart, Lord
Mayor of the City of London, 1762.*

I find this an interesting addition to the hors d'oeuvres tray, or a
new cocktail tit-bit. The *tour de main du chef* is the sliced ginger, but
only fresh 'green' ginger, of course.

CAVEACH OR PICKLED MACKEREL

"Take 6 large mackerel, cut them into round pieces. Have
ready 1oz Pepper, 3 large Nutmegs some mace and a handful of Salt. Mix these together and having made 2 or 3
holes in each piece of fish, put into them the seasoning—
thrusting it in sufficiently—and rub as well each piece
over with the same—fry them brown in oil, then let them
stand to be cold—put them into Vinegar and cover them
with oil—they are delicious eating—and—if they be well
covered—they will keep a long time."

*The London Art of Cookery, and Housekeeper's Complete Assistant On
a New Plan. Made Plain and Easy to the Understanding of every*

Housekeeper, Cook, and Servant in the Kingdom. By John Farley, Principal Cook at the London Tavern. Original edition 1783, *reprinted* 12 *times, last edition* 1811.

There are many receipts for Caveach to be found in eighteenth- and early nineteenth-century cookery books and I have selected this as one of the simplest. The method was also applied to herring, soles and other fish. A few incisions with a knife to rub in the spices are preferable to making the prescribed 'holes', and not having the extreme addiction to quantities of nutmeg so much favoured by eighteenth-century cooks, I cut this down to sensible proportions. Another author dealing with Caveach in quantity 'for persons at sea', recommends sliced onion or shallot between layers in a barrel.

I concur with John Farley in describing it as delicious, and a welcome change from the more familiar soused mackerel with which it has some affinity. I found a very similar dish in a restaurant in Hamburg some years ago, where the menu described it as *Nach Hausfrauen Art.*

(To satisfy the curious, the name itself derives from *escabeche,* the Spanish for pickled fish, easily corrupted in our own tongue to caveach).

TO STEW HERRINGS

"First broil them very brown, then have ready some White-wine made hot with an Anchovy, a blade of Mace, and a bit of Onion, with a little whole Pepper, all stew'd in the Wine; then cut off the Heads of the Fish, and bruise them in the Wine and Spice, and take them out again before you put in your Herrings; let them stew over Coals, in a Dish that they may lie at length in; let them stew on both sides, 'till they are enough at the Bone; take them out, and shake up the Sauce with Butter and Flower. 'Tis a very good Way to Dress them."

A Collection of Above Three Hundred Receipts in Cookery, Physick and Surgery; For the Use of all Good Wives, Tender Mothers, and Careful Nurses. By several Hands. London. Printed for Richard Wilkin, at the King's Head in St Paul's Church-yard. MDCCXIV.

The term 'stew' has other, perhaps less toothsome, connotations today, and if you are going to present this to your guests, I would suggest an alternative title; having regard to the wine content I called it Tippled Herring, but you may have a better name.

The dish is really an elaboration of herring cooked *au court bouillon*, but the subtlety is provided in grilling the fish and thickening the sauce.

A better procedure is to have the herrings filleted, with the skin left on, but bring back the heads and bones (and a few more begged from the fishmonger).

Prepare your basic sauce with ½ pint of dry white wine, or wine and water, 2 crushed anchovy fillets, a pinch of ground mace, a few peppercorns, and a small onion grated. Bring to the boil, and then allow to simmer while you get the herrings ready anointed with butter or oil on both sides. Grill them skin side up. When they are well cooked, strain the sauce-base into a shallow fireproof dish, lay in the herrings and allow to heat through in the oven for a few minutes to take up the wine. Before serving, pour off the sauce, thicken with flour and butter, and serve separately.

FISH RECHAUFFÉ

"After pike, skate, cod-fish, turbot, or any other solid fish has been boiled, pick it from the bones & skin it very clean in small flakes or bits, to one pound of fish so picked add ½ pint of cream, a tablespoonfull of mushroom catsup, a tablespoonfull of anchovy liquor, a little cayenne pepper, flour and butter; make it quite hot in a saucepan and then put it in a dish, put grated bread over it, and moisten the crumbs with oiled-butter; then brown with a Salamander just before it is served up. Half a pound of fish is sufficient for two persons."

MS Family Cook Book. Loaned by Miss Hull.

Our forefathers were evidently unaware (happily for them) of the dreary confection known in all families as 'fish-cakes'. This version is far more palatable, and, for the calorie-conscious, is bereft of potato. 'Anchovy liquor' presented some difficulty and in my version I substitute a *tea*spoonful of anchovy essence. Mushroom ketchup can be bought, and the flour and butter flavoured with a drop or two of tabasco. Otherwise I followed the directions and finally browned it under the grill. Garnish with chopped parsley and watercress for special occasions

TO MAKE A VIRGINIA TROUT

"Take Pickled Herrings, cut off their Heads, lay the bodies two dayes and nights in Water, then wash them well, then season them with Mace, Cinamon, Cloves Pepper and a little Red Saunders, then lay them close in a pot with a little onion strowed small upon them and cast between every layer; when you have thus done, put in a pint of Clarret-Wine to them, and cover them with double paper tyed on the pot, and set them in the oven with househould bread. They are to be eaten cold."

The Compleat Cook. Expertly prescribing the most ready wayes for dressing of Flesh, and Fish, ordering of Sauces or Making of Pastry. London. Printed by E.B. for Nath Brook at the Angel in Cornhill, 1658.

Those with a taste for Dutch *matjes* herring and roll-mops may like to try this interesting variation. 'Red Saunders' at first defied definition, until a chance reference to the OED revealed them as dye manufactured from the bark of a tree related to sandalwood. We would induce a pink tint with cochineal, but the red wine will colour the fish sufficiently to give the illusion of salmon-trout for which the anonymous author was striving. His cooking instruction refers to a bread oven, so that it would have cooked while the loaves were baking. I simply placed the cooking jar containing the spiced and anointed fish in a pan of water in a brisk oven for 40 minutes. For 3 pickled herring less than $\frac{1}{2}$ pint of red wine was enough.

SALMON PIE

"Having made a good crust, cleanse a piece of salmon well, season it with salt, mace and nutmeg, a piece of butter at the bottom of the dish, and lay your salmon in. Melt butter according to your pie. Take a lobster, boil it, pick out all the flesh, chop it small, bruise the body, and mix it well with the butter. Pour it over your salmon, put on the lid, and bake it well."

The London Art of Cookery, and Housekeeper's Complete Assistant. On a New Plan. Made Plain and Easy to the Understanding of every Housekeeper, Cook, and Servant in the Kingdom. By John Farley, Principal Cook at the London Tavern. Original edition 1783, *reprinted* 12 *times, last edition* 1811.

Those who may have other use for these costly ingredients may like to try a poor man's version which I find quite successful. Use the contents of a can of good quality red salmon, including the liquor, and for the lobster substitute the picked meat of a freshly-boiled crab. A dusting of paprika before closing the pie gives it a good finish, and it will bake in about an hour in a moderate oven.

Meat and Poultry

TO MAKE STEWED STEAKES

"Take a peece of Mutton, and cutte it into peeces, and wash it very cleane, and put it into a faire potte with Ale or with halfe Wine, then make it boyle, and skumme it cleyne, and put into your pot a faggot of Rosemary and Time, then take some Parseley picked fine, and some onyons cut round, and let them all boyle together, then take prunes, and raisons, dates and currans, and let it boyle together, and season it with Sinnamon and Ginger, Nutmeggs, two or three Cloves and Salt, and so serve it on Soppes and garnish it with fruite."

The Good Huswifes Jewell 1585. *By Thomas Dawson, wherein is to be found most excellent and rare Devises for conceites in Cookery, found out by the practise of Thomas Dawson.*

————————————————

I have included this rather exotic (and breathless) receipt because when I first discovered it (in the British Museum Library) I experienced a feeling of *déjà vu*, although this was one of very few extant copies and it was impossible that I had read it elsewhere. The idea persisted, however, and after looking through a few likely sources in

47

my own possession I recognised as almost identical a recipe given in Claudia Roden's *A Book of Middle Eastern Food* (published Thomas Nelson 1968, Penguin Books 1970) which I quote here *in toto* with due acknowledgements to the source.

Moroccan Tagine with Quince

"2lb fat or lean stewing lamb, cubed: 2 onions finely chopped: salt and pepper: 1 bunch fresh coriander or parsley, finely chopped: $\frac{1}{4}$ teaspoon powdered saffron [optional]: $\frac{1}{2}$ teaspoon ground ginger: $\frac{1}{2}$–$1\frac{1}{2}$lb quinces cut in half and cored but not peeled: (here she adds a note: you may prefer to use less fruit the first time you try this dish. Increase the amount once you have become accustomed to the taste of the meat flavoured with the sweet aromas of the fruit, and the sharp shock of quince with ginger. Some people prefer to soften the taste of quince with a little sugar): 2oz butter [optional].

"Put the cubed meat and 1 chopped onion in a large saucepan. Cover with water and season to taste with salt and pepper.... Add fresh coriander or parsley, saffron if used, and ginger, bring to the boil and simmer gently, covered, until the meat is tender and the onion has practically disintegrated in the sauce. This takes about an hour. Now add the other chopped onion and cook until soft. Half an hour before serving add the quinces and cook until only just tender. The quinces may be sautéed in butter first for a richer flavour.

"Pears or apples (peeled and cored) *dates and raisins* [my italics] or prunes may be used instead of the quinces, sometimes in combinations. They all make rather luxurious dishes. Chicken is also delicious cooked in this way."

The close similarity seems to me to be more than coincidental. Trade with the Middle East was certainly flourishing in the Eliza-bethan economy, and it seems likely that the predilection for sweet additions to meat may well have had its origins from the merchant adventurers whose ships carried this commerce. A more romantic speculation is that perhaps old Master Dawson had among his circle of friends some old sea-captain who had experienced captivity among the dreaded Algerine Corsairs or Barbary pirates, and at whose table he was a sometime guest. But that is another story. Of course the Moslem recipe eschews 'halfe wine' which I use (with water) and find good.

BEEF TREMBLONQUE

"Tie up closely the fat end of a brisket of beef. Put it into a pot of water, and boil it six hours very gently. Season the water with a little salt, a handfull of allspice, two onions, two turnips, and a carrot. In the mean time, put a piece of butter into a stew-pan, and melt it. Then put in two spoonfuls of flour, and stir it till it be smooth. Put in a quart of gravy, a spoonful of catchup, the same of browning, a gill of white wine, turnips and carrots, and cut them as for harrico of mutton. Stew them gently till the roots be tender, and season with pepper and salt. Skim the fat clean off, put the beef in the dish, and pour the sauce over it. Garnish with pickles of any sort. If you choose it, you may make a sauce thus: Chop a handful of parsley, one onion, four pickled cucumbers, one walnut, and a gill of capers. Put them into a pint of good gravy, and thicken it with a little butter rolled in flour; season it with pepper and salt, and boil it up for ten minutes. Put the beef in a dish, with greens and carrots round it."

The London Art of Cookery, and Housekeeper's Complete Assistant. On a New Plan. Made Plain and Easy to the Understanding of every

Housekeeper, Cook, and Servant in the Kingdom. By John Farley, Principal Cook at the London Tavern. Original edition 1783, *reprinted* 12 *times, last edition* 1811.

Customers at The London Tavern who were doubtless regaled on this sophisticated version of boiled beef and carrots probably preferred, as I did, the second sauce. Rolled and tied brisket is inclined to be fat (he even specifies the fat end) and a sharp sauce is indicated. The ingredients should be well chopped (don't omit the walnut) and served piping hot.

A VERY PRETTY WAY TO EAT COLD BOILED BEEF

"Slice it as thin as 'tis possible, Slice also an onion, or a shallot, and squeeze on it the juice of a lemon or two, then beat it between two plates, as you do cucumbers; when 'tis very well beaten and tastes sharp of the lemon, put into a deep china dish, pick out the onion, and pour on oil, shake in also some shred parsley, and garnish with sliced lemon; 'tis very savoury and delicious."

A Collection of Above Three Hundred Receipts in Cookery, Physick and Surgery, 1715. *By Mary Kittelby.*

This book went through seven editions (the last, 1759). The authoress recommends her book to the Clergy 'especially to those whose Parishes are remote from other Help'. Indeed, what better advice to Help a Hot and Costive Habit of Body than this?

'Roasted Apples with Carroway Comfits, eaten constantly every Night, has been the Method of a Gentleman of Fourscore, who has hardly ever taken other Physick, or omitted this for Fifty years, and

Page 51 'Convenience' foods have arrived (1852). Ritchie and M'Call's canning factory in Houndsditch, London. The beginning of the end . . . .

Page 52   *Roasting the baron of beef at the Lord Mayor's Banquet, 1847. Note the turnspit at top left*

never felt the Gout, or Stone, or any other Distemper incident to Old Age.'

As the plates were probably pewter, you will not want to beat your kitchen crockery. But you can press it in gently, or beat it on a board.

A salad to accompany, of course.

BAKED MUTTON CHOPS

"Cut a neck or loin of mutton into steaks, put some salt and pepper on it; butter the dish and lay your steaks in it; then take a quart of milk, six eggs beat fine, and a small quantity of flour, put in a little beaten ginger and some salt. Pour this over the steaks, and send it to the oven. It will take about half an hour's baking."

The London Cook, or the Whole Art of Cookery Made Easy and Familiar, by William Gelleroy, Late Cook to her Grace the Dutchess of Argyle. And now to the Right Hon Sir Samuel Fludyer Bart, Lord Mayor of the City of London, 1762.

As you are unlikely to use a whole loin, and it is more likely to be lamb, take ½ pint of milk and 2 eggs with a teaspoonful of flour for 4 chops. The pinch of powdered ginger can be varied with a mild curry powder.

TO DRESS HOGS-FEET AND EARS, THE BEST WAY

"When they are nicely clean'd, put them into a Pot, with a Bay-leaf, and a large Onion, and as much Water as will cover them; season it with Salt and a little Pepper; bake them with Household-Bread; keep them in this Pickle 'till you want them, then take them out and cut them in handsome pieces; fry them, and take for Sauce three spoon-fulls of the Pickle; shake in some Flower, a piece of Butter, and a spoon-full of Mustard: Lay the Ears in the middle, the Feet round, and pour the Sauce over."

A Collection of Above Three Hundred Receipts in Cookery, Physick and Surgery; For the Use of all Good Wives, Tender Mothers, and Careful Nurses. By several Hands. London, Printed for Richard Wilkin, at the King's Head in St Paul's Church-yard. MDCCXIV.

On this side of the Channel, pig's ears rarely make an appearance in the butcher's shop, save those attached the head which we use for home-made brawn. The French know better, and they are to be found in various items of *charcuterie*, particularly the wonderful galantine they call *hure*. So perforce we must make do with pig's trotters, which are cheap and easily obtainable.

My original experiment with this proved an abject failure due, I think, to the author's directions for a watery 'pickle'. The general treatment, however, seemed interesting, and I was later rewarded with the discovery of the following, in Richard Dolby's *Cook's Dictionary* (1830).

"Having cleaned the feet, put a bottle of white wine to three pairs of feet and ears, some bay leaves and a bunch of sweet herbs. Let them boil gently until tender, then take them out of the liquor, lay them in an earthen pan; when cold, take off the fat, and strain the liquor over them. They eat well cold or warmed in the jelly thickened with butter rolled in flour."

54

I split the feet, and simmered them gently for nearly 3 hours in half the quantity of wine, with a little water. Reverting to the original receipt, I added a teaspoon of mustard to the sauce, which gives it a necessary piquancy.

VEAL SWEETBREAD LIKE HEDGEHOGS

"Scald the sweetbreads, and lard them with ham and truffles, cut in small lardons, and fried for a short time in butter (lard them so that the lardons may stick out a little to give the appearance of bristles): simmer the sweetbread thus larded in the same butter the lardons were fried in, with stock, a glass of white wine, seasoned with a little salt, and pepper; when done, skim and strain the sauce, add a little cullis, and serve this over the sweetbreads."

The Cook's Dictionary, and Housekeeper's Directory: A New Family Manual of Cookery and Confectionery, on A Plan of Ready Reference Never Hitherto attempted. By Richard Dolby, Late Cook at The Thatched House Tavern, St James's Street. 1st edition 1830.

This, of course, calls for larding needles, which are now easy to obtain and simple to use. Once again we must perforce omit the truffles, but ham cut in Julienne strips looks and tastes good by itself. I thickened the sauce with a little arrowroot, and displayed the resulting dish to my guests as a *tour de force* of culinary one-upmanship.

NEAT'S TONGUE PUDDING

"Boil your tongues very tender, then peel and slice them, and beat them in a mortar, till they are a paste, then put to them some cream, the yolks of eggs well beaten, some grated bread, salt, sugar, grated nutmeg, and mace to your taste, and as much marrow as you think will make them fat enough; so fill some skins clean washed, and boil them, and serve them with melted butter."

The London Cook, or the Whole Art of Cookery Made Easy and Familiar, by William Gelleroy, Late Cook to her Grace the Dutchess of Argyle. And now to the Right Hon Sir Samuel Fludyer Bart, Lord Mayor of the City of London, 1762.

In common, I suspect, with most readers, I found difficulty in following this receipt exactly, because of the difficulty of finding 'skins clean washed' into which sausages were once filled. So unless you have a kindly country butcher, try it this way:

For 4 people you will require 3 smallish calves tongues (without the roots); 4 eggs, a gill of cream, a good handful of breadcrumbs, and the suggested seasonings to taste. Instead of sugar I used a glass of sweet white wine, and for the beef marrow I substituted pork fat from a trimmed chop, but possibly a little suet would serve.

Put the boiled and skinned tongues through the mincer, add the other ingredients, including some milled black pepper, and place the mixture in the blender briefly. Put the resultant mixture in a terrine, or shallow oven-proof dish, cover with foil, stand it in a baking tin filled with water. Cook in a slow oven for ¾ of an hour. I found a little horseradish in the melted butter (see 'Melted Butter', p 155) just the right sauce. If left to cool, this makes an admirable *pâté*.

TO MAKE FRENCH-CUTLETS, VERY GOOD

"Skin a Loin of Mutton, and cut it into Stakes, then take some of the lean of a Leg of Veal, the weight in Beef-suet, two Anchovies, Thyme, Parsly, Sweet-marjoram and Onion, all finely shred; Nutmeg, Pepper, Salt and grated Bread, with the Yolks of two Eggs; make holes in the lean of the Stakes and fill them full of this Seasoning, and spread it all over the Stakes, then butter as many pieces of white Paper as you have Cutlets, and wrap them up every one by themselves, turn up the edges of the Papers with great care that none of the Moisture get out; therefore let the Papers be large enough to turn up several times at the edge; and if occasion be, stick a pin to keep it all in; for this Gravy is all their Sauce: When they are thus tight wrapt up, put them upon a Mazareen, and bake them: When they are enough, take them off the Dish they were baked on, and put them on a clean hot Dish; do not take off the Papers but serve them in as they were baked: This is a very delicious Savory Dish, and done with little danger of spoiling, if you wrap them up close. Many People like these best without Sauce; but if you chuse it, let it be strong Gravy, Spice, Onion, shred Capers, Juice of Lemon shook up with a bit of Butter; but they are savory and most wholesome alone."

A Collection of Above Three Hundred Receipts in Cookery, Physick and Surgery; For the Use of all Good Wives, Tender Mothers, and Careful Nurses. By several Hands. London, Printed for Richard Wilkin, at the King's Head in St Paul's Church-yard. MDCCXIV.

This dish adapts well to the modern kitchen, and is a pleasant and easy alternative to your workaday grilled lamb chops. Take as many chops as you require, trim them, and prepare a stuffing with minced veal, or any other your butcher can provide, if you don't want the trouble of preparation. It will have enough fat without the addition of suet. Bind it with egg, breadcrumbs and spices, but use the anchovies and forget the salt. The 'holes in the lean' appear superfluous, but score the chops lightly if you wish to allow the flavour to penetrate.

In today's terms we can use foil wrapping instead of buttered white paper, which eliminates the necessity for a pin! Spread the stuffing exactly as specified, and place them in an ovenware dish. (For the curious, by a 'mazareen' was meant a deep pewter plate.) Twenty-five minutes in a brisk oven is about 'enough'. I served them with caper sauce, handed separately, and agreed with the anonymous authors that it proved both delicious and savoury.

MUTTON KEBOBBED

"Take a loin of mutton, and joint it between every bone, and put between every bone a slice of apple, and a slice of onion, season it with pepper and salt moderately, grate a small nutmeg all over, dip them in the yolks of three eggs, and have ready crumbs of bread and sweet herbs, and dip them in and clap them together in the same shape again, and put it on a small spit, roast them before a quick fire, set a dish under, and baste it with a little piece of butter, and then keep basting with what comes from it, and throw some crumbs of bread all over them as it is a roasting; when it is enough take it up, and lay it in the dish, and have ready half a pint of good gravy, and what comes from it, take two spoonfuls of ketchup, and mix a tea spoonful of flour with it and put to the gravy, stir it together, and give it a boil and pour over the mutton. Note: You must observe to take off the fat of the inside and the skin off the top of the meat, and some of the fat, if there be too much; when you put in what comes from your meat into the gravy, observe to pour out all the fat."

The London Cook, or the Whole Art of Cookery Made Easy and Familiar, by William Gelleroy, Late Cook to her Grace the Dutchess of Argyle. And now to the Right Hon Sir Samuel Fludyer Bart, Lord Mayor of the City of London, 1762.

Get the butcher to chine the joint, and when dividing the chops, don't quite sever the connection with the backbone. If you don't possess an electric spit, tie the loin together with string (having 'clapped' it in shape), brush with egg and herby breadcrumbs and roast in the ordinary way. I'm not sure about pouring the gravy-sauce over it. To my mind it spoils the crisp brown top. Yours is the decision.

A HAM PYE

"Slice some cold boiled ham about half an inch thick, make a good crust, and thick, over the dish, and lay a layer of ham, shake a little pepper over it, then take a large young fowl clean picked, gutted, washed and singed; put a little pepper and salt in the belly, and rub a very little salt on the outside; lay the fowl on the ham, boil some eggs hard, put in the yolks, and cover all with ham, then shake some pepper on the ham, and put on the top-crust. Bake it well, have ready when it comes out of the oven some very rich beef-gravy, enough to fill the pye, lay on the crust again, and send it to the table hot. A fresh ham will not be so tender; so that I always boil my ham one day, and bring it to table, and the next day make a pye of it. It does better than an unboiled ham. If you put two large fowls in they will make a fine pye, but that is according to your company, more or less. The crust must be the same you make for a venison pasty. You should pour a little strong gravy into the pye when you bake it, just to bake the meat, and then fill it up when it comes out of the oven. Boil some truffles and morels, and put into the pye, it is a great addition; and fresh mushrooms or dried ones."

The London Cook, or the Whole Art of Cookery Made Easy and Familiar, by William Gelleroy, Late Cook to her Grace the Dutchess of Argyle. And now to the Right Hon Sir Samuel Fludyer Bart, Lord Mayor of the City of London, 1762.

I found this a good way to finish the left-over portion of a piece of boiling bacon, which answers just as well as expensive gammon. In a deep earthenware casserole lined with your pastry put a double layer of thinly sliced bacon, dust with milled pepper and a sprinkling of chopped parsley. On this put your prepared chicken (not necessarily a large one!) with the hard-boiled eggs, whole if you like, and a bare $\frac{1}{2}$ pint of gravy (or concentrated chicken stock from a cube). Use the rest of your available bacon to cover the chicken, put on the crust and bake in a well-heated oven until the pastry has risen and set. Finish in a moderate heat and pour in the rich gravy or stock as advised. Or, if you can take the trouble, use the Lear for Savoury Pies on p 166 Total time, about 2 hours, depending on the size of your bird. Note the suggestion of dried mushrooms, which have more flavour than fresh.

A LAMB PYE

"Cut a hind quarter of lamb into thin slices; season it with savoury spice, and lay them in the pye with a hard lettuce and artichoke bottoms, the tops of an hundred of asparagus: Lay on butter, and close the pye. When it is baked, pour into it a lear."

The Compleat Housewife or Accomplish'd Gentlewoman's Companion, 15th edition, 1753. By Eliza Smith.

For the 'savoury spice' I used ground allspice (what the French term *quatre épices*, and assert has the flavour of clove, nutmeg, cinnamon and pepper).

The 'hundred asparagus' obviously presents a problem, and in any case was probably the thin growth marketed as 'sprues'. A can of green asparagus tips, with the liquor, makes an admirable substitute, and similarly, of course, with artichoke bottoms.

TO BOIL SMOAKED FLESH

"Mounsieur Overbec doth tell me, that when He boileth a Gambon of Bacon, or any salted flesh and hanged in the smoak (as Neats-tongues, Hung-beef, and Hogs-cheeks, &c), He putteth into the Kettle of water to boil with them three or four handfuls of *fleur de foin*, (more or less according to the quantity of flesh and water), tyed loosly in a bag of course-cloth. This maketh it much tenderer, shorter, mellower, and of a finer colour."

The Closet of the Eminently Learned Sir Kenelm Digby, Kt, Opened. 1669.

Here is the much-travelled writer again subtly drawing his readers' attention to his continental connections. But in fact this method of cooking hams has been regularly used by farmers' wives in Kent, and doubtless elsewhere, for centuries, and it was from them that I learnt this culinary hint of improving the flavour with a wisp of hay in the water.

TO JUG A KNUCKEL OF VEAL

"Put ye veal into a jug wth a bit of beef 2 or 3 heads of
endive 2 or 3 oinions, salery & mace ½ a pint of water,
thyme, parsley, peper & salt, cover it close & boil it in a pot
3 hours then take it out & dish it up, fling out ye parsly &
thyme and serve away hot."

*From the Brotherton Library MSS Collection, University of Leeds
MS 53. (Circa 1720.)*

This method of cooking the knuckle may well, in the seventeenth
century, have been the best means of slow cooking, ie in an earthenware vessel placed in an iron cooking pot, suspended from a pot-hook
or crane over the open fire. Today, with regulated heat, this is no
longer a problem. Have your knuckle either sawn in several pieces by
the butcher, or remove some of the meatier part if you cook it whole.
Place it in a stewpan or casserole with about ¼lb of diced pickled pork
(rather than beef) with the vegetables and herbs as given; bring it to
the boil in as much water as will cover it, add a few peppercorns and a
scant teaspoon of coarse salt, skim, and reduce the heat to give a
gentle simmer. Cover, and allow the 3 hours to cook. I see no reason
to 'fling out' the herbs, but if you are using a *bouquet garni*, remove
this before serving with parsley butter (qv). To give additional zest put
in a good strip of lemon peel to cook with the meat.

TO STEW A BREST OF VEAL

"Half roast it, take a little strong broth, put to it a little
ale, mace, peper, anchovy, sweet herbs stew ye veal in it,
take cockles, pickels, lemon peel, mushrooms, & capers

shred 'em together melt $\frac{1}{2}$e of butter & wⁿ yᵉ veals enough,
put yᵉ pickels into yᵉ butter & dish it up cover it wᵗʰ fry'd
sweetbreds & lemon."

*From the Brotherton Library MSS Collection, University of Leeds.
MS 53. (Circa* 1720.)

The adaptation I found the simplest for 2 to 3 lb of breast of veal
was to first brown it well in butter and oil mixed, cooking the mushrooms with it. Remove the joint to the stewpan in which you have put
$\frac{1}{2}$ pint of stock or good beef consommé (canned) and a glass of white
wine (instead of ale); season it as directed, crushing or chopping 2
anchovy fillets and tying a faggot of herbs, or a muslin bag of *bouquet
garni*. Cover the pan and allow to simmer gently for at least $1\frac{1}{2}$ hours,
or until the meat is tender. Meanwhile prepare your sharp sauce by
thickening about 6oz of butter with a little flour and a further glass of
wine or stock and heat up the cockles (bottled are best for this), a
chopped gherkin, a very little lemon peel, capers and the cooked
mushrooms. The fried sweetbreads are a refinement you may wish to
omit, but they enhance the finished dish considerably.

BORDYKE VEAL CAKE

"Take a pound and a half of veal perfectly clear of fat and
skin, and eight ounces of the nicest striped bacon; chop
them separately, then mix them well together with the
grated rind of a small lemon, half a teaspoonful of salt, a
fourth as much of cayenne, the third part of a nutmeg
and a half-teaspoonful of freshly pounded mace. When it is
pressed into the dish, let it be somewhat higher in the
centre than at the edge; and whether to be served hot or

cold, lift it out as soon as it comes from the oven, and place
it on a strainer that the fat may drain from it; it will keep
many days if the under side be dry. The bacon should be
weighed after the rind, and any rust it may exhibit, have
been trimmed from it. This cake is excellent cold; slices,
if preferred hot, may be warmed through in a Dutch
oven, or on the gridiron, or in a few spoonsful of gravy.
The same ingredients made into small cakes, well
floured, and slowly fried from twelve to fifteen minutes,
then served with gravy made in the pan as for cutlets, will
be found extremely good. Veal, 1½lb; striped bacon, 8
oz; salt and mace, 1 teaspoonful each; rind of lemon, 1;
third of 1 nutmeg; cayenne, 4 grains; baked 1¼ to 1½
hour."

*Modern Cookery, for Private Families, Reduced to a System of Easy
Practice, 1845. By Eliza Acton.*
    This work, which was extremely popular, running into many edi-
tions, was heavily plagiarised by Mrs Beeton (1859) to the point
where the author's copy (1878) contains in the preface the following
passage: 'At the risk of appearing extremely egotistic, I have appended
"Author's Receipt" . . . to many of the contents; but I have done it
solely in self-defence, in consequence of the unscrupulous manner in
which large portions of my volume have been appropriated by contemporary authors without the slightest acknowledgment. . . .'

'Striped' is what we term streaky bacon. Chopping is laborious and
makes a rather coarse cake. Try it minced, not too fine. What is sold
as stewing veal is perfectly adequate, and a glass of dry white wine will
finish it nicely.

TO MAKE CECILS

"Mince any kind of cold meat add crumbs of bread a little
chopped Onion a little Lemon peel grated or cut fine half
an Anchovy chopped small a little pepper and salt and
nutmeg and a little butter—make it hot on the fire and stir
it well then put in the yolk of an egg well beaten make it
up with a little flour into balls dip them into the white of
an Egg with bread crumbs in it and fry them a light brown
—pour a little brown Gravy over them—Miss Ann
Penkett 1800."

Amy Hull Family MS Receipt Book. Loaned by Miss Hull.

For jaded palates, try this with the addition of a little curry powder
or paprika, or substitute a thick cheese sauce for the 'brown Gravy'.

A POUPETON

"Mince a fillet of veal very small wth ye same quantity of
beef suit beat it in a marter wth a raw egg or 2 to bind it
season it wth savory spice make it in ye form of a thick
round pye & fill it thus, put in thin slices of bacon,
squab'd pidgeons, sliced sweet breads, shiverd pallets,
cocks combs boild & blanchd, & a little butter, close it up
wth forc'd meat as a pie wash it over batter of eggs &
bake it."

*From the Brotherton Library MSS Collection, University of Leeds.
MS 53. (Circa 1720.)*

As the fillet is expensive, use any cheaper cut of veal. I used what is sold as 'pie veal', with its attendant fat, omitted the suet, and put 2lb through the mincer twice. Season it well, adding a few mixed herbs to the spices, which should include a pinch of ground ginger. Bind the whole with egg and line a round pie dish with this; then put in the parboiled sweetbreads which you have previously prepared, six or seven rashers of streaky bacon, and the breast of a pigeon if you are adventurous; the shivered palates (sliced ox palates) and cocks' combs can be safely omitted. Add a large knob of butter, cover with the remaining mince and brush over well with the egg batter as instructed Give it a good hour in a moderate oven.

WHITE SCOTCH COLLOPS

"Cut ye veal in peices about ye bigness of a goos quil beat it wth ye back of a knife take a pint of cream some marjoram, nutmeg, & mace, put ye collops in & let 'em lie all night fry 'em in butter, don't drain 'em from ye cream a little time will fry 'em, make ye sause wth gravey of veal, mace, anchovey & a little lemon squeez'd boil it ye sause pan take ye collops out & put ye sause into ye pan wth some butter lay forc'd meat balls over ye collops & pour in ye sause garnish wth balls lemon & slices of bacon, boil ye bacon a little & crisp it before ye fire."

From the Brotherton Library MSS collection, University of Leeds MS 53. (Circa 1720.)

The frequent appearance of Scotch Collops in the old kitchens bears no special Caledonian significance. It is, in fact, an etymological perversion of scotched, or sliced, collops, which were simply pieces of meat (not necessarily veal—see Lady Diana Porter's receipt, below and the method of preparation varied widely.

In this version, long narrow strips of veal are called for, beaten flat like small *escalopes*, with which word it possibly has some affinity. Marinade overnight half a dozen of these in a ½ pint of cream and milk mixed, with a teaspoon of marjoram and a scant dusting of nutmeg and ground mace. The following day put the marinade in a shallow stewpan with a knob of butter and cook the veal strips until tender—about 10 minutes. Meanwhile, in another pan prepare the sauce; make a white *roux* (with about an ounce of butter and slightly less flour) over gentle heat, and pour on a cupful of seasoned stock with a teaspoon of anchovy essence and a squeeze of lemon, stirring continually until boiling. The garnish of forcemeat balls certainly gives the dish a finish and can be made simply with 1oz butter, 1 shallot finely chopped with a little parsley, a pinch of sage and 4oz breadcrumbs, all mixed, bound with egg, and fried in deep fat. Omit these if you will, but include the crisped streaky bacon and lemon quarters.

MY LADY DIANA PORTER'S SCOTCH COLLOPS

"Cut a leg or two of Mutton into thin slices, which beat very well. Put them to fry over a very quick fire in a pan first glased over, with no more Butter melted in it, then just to besmear a little all the bottom of the Pan. Turn them in due time. There must never be but one row in the pan, nor any slice lying upon another; but every one immediate to the pan. When they are fryed enough, lay them in a hot dish covered, over a Chafing-dish, and pour upon them the Gravy that run out of them into the Pan. Then lay another row of slices in the Pan to fry as before; and when they are enough, put them into the dish to the other. When you have enough, by such repetitions, or by

67

doing them in two or three pans, all at a time; take a Porrenger full of Gravy of Mutton, and put into it a piece of Butter as much a Wall-nut, and a quartered Onion if you will (or rub the dish afterwards with Garlike) and Pepper and Salt, and let this boil to be very hot; then throw away the Onion, and pour this into the dish upon the slices, and let them stew a little together; then squeeze an Orange upon it, and serve it up."

The Closet of the Eminently Learned Sir Kenelm Digby, Kt, Opened. 1669.

As in his receipt for 'Savoury Collops', the author again uses orange juice to finish his dish. I tried this with 4 slices from the fillet end of a half leg of lamb cut about $\frac{1}{2}$in thick, so as to fit into a large frying-pan. The charred outside, and succulent, slightly pink inside which resulted seemed not to call for a 'Porrenger' of gravy, so while they were cooking I dusted them with garlic salt and served them simply in their own juices, with new potatoes and watercress, and a final squeeze of orange. But if you feel a sauce is necessary I suggest using the one called *marchand des vins*, which is not entirely dissimilar. I make it thus:

Sweat 2 heaped tablespoonfuls of chopped onion in a similar amount of butter for a few minutes; add a gill of red wine and the same amount of stock and reduce until thickened. Remove from heat and stir in 2oz of butter, a little chopped parsley, and salt and pepper to taste. Pour over the lamb steaks (which you have kept hot) and serve.

A FLORENDINE MAGISTRAL

"Cut thin slices of a leg of veal, like Scotch collops, beat them with a knife on both sides; season them with salt,

Page 69 *Stove, oven and spit at the Great Exhibition,* 1851

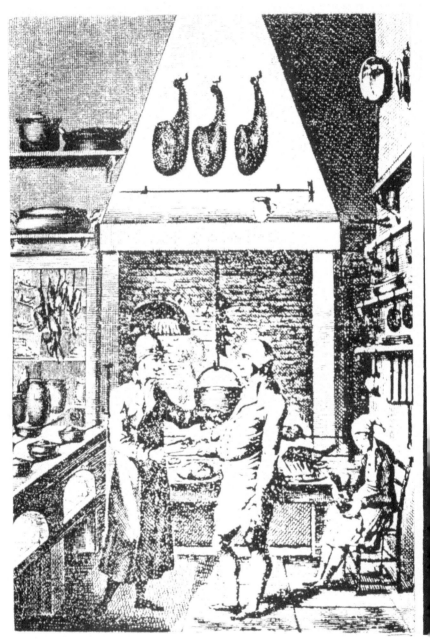

Page 70 *Instructions to the cook in an eighteenth-century kitchen. On the left is the warmer for soups and sauces*

pepper, cloves and mace. Cut as many thin slices of fat bacon, roll them up and put them into your pye-dish. Add two or three shalots, and two or three anchovies, some oysters, and forty or fifty forced-meat balls, and lemon par'd and slic'd; put in a quarter of a pint of gravy, half a pint of strong broth, and half a pint of white wine; cover it with puff-paste and bake it."

The London Cook, or the Whole Art of Cookery Made Easy and Familiar, by William Gelleroy, Late Cook to her Grace the Dutchess of Argyle. And now to the Right Hon Sir Samuel Fludyer Bart, Lord Mayor of the City of London, 1762.

SAVOURY COLLOPS OF VEAL

"Cut a Leg of Veal into thin Collops, and beat them well with the back of a Knife. Then lay them in soak a good half hour in the yolks of four eggs, and the whites of two very well beaten, and a little small shreded Thyme mingled with it; then lay them in the Frying-pan, wherein is boiling Butter, and pour upon them the rest of the Eggs, that the Collops have not Imbibed, and carry with them, and fry them very well, turning them in due time. Then pour away all the Butter, and make them a Sauce of Gravy seasoned with Salt and Spice, and juyce of Orange at last squeesed upon them."

The Closet of the Eminently Learned Sir Kenelm Digby, Kt, Opened. 1669.

When you are tired of breaded veal cutlets and escalopes, this is worth trying, if only for the novelty of tasting the eighteenth-century addiction to the flavour of orange juice with meat where we favour lemon.

FORCED MEAT BALLS FOR SCOTCH COLLOPS OR RAGGUE OR CALFS HEAD HASH

"Take veale and pick it from all ye sinues and skins and to halfe a pound of Veale take ye liek quantity of good beefe suit and for want of that ye may use ye Kele (caul, Ed.) of y^r Veale if it be not too skeney. Cut and shred y^r meat very fine, then have some sweet hearbes as Lemon Time Sweet Marjoram a few Leaves of Sage and a little Parsley a Leek blad or a few chives so as and shred those season y^r meat with a little peper nutmeg and salt y^n put y^r hearbes to it then have sume grated stale whit bread about 3 spoon fulls mix with ye rest then beat one Egg and put to ye rest mix ale well together y^n make it in to balls about ye bigness of a wall nut or scarse so big fry y^m and when fryed take sume of y^m and shake in y^r sause and Lay y^m upon y^r meat."

Captain Thomas Pownall's Book, 1688. *John Hodgkin. From the Brotherton Library MSS collection, University of Leeds. MS 45, ff 38, 60.*

This book has a curious history, being the log-book of a troop of Dragoons touring the country for an unspecified purpose during 1688–9. In it are entered the names of places where they stopped, and the receipts of the various innkeepers who quartered them, with bills for feeding man and horse (meat, horsemeat and drinke).

Last entry, in the City of Lincoln, is a receipt for 37 days Quarter, signed by the Mayor. Somehow it was left behind and the many spare pages utilised by some unknown thrifty Lincolnshire housewife for entering her cooking receipts.

8oz pie veal; 8oz shredded suet; the named herbs *à discretion* ('ware too much Sage!) pepper, salt, nutmeg to taste, 3 dessertspoonfuls of stale breadcrumbs; 1 egg. Mince the meat content, and blend in the herbs and spices with the well-beaten egg. Roll the mixture with floured hands into small balls and fry them in lard or deep fat.

These forcemeat balls were extremely popular in the seventeenth and eighteenth century, to give a zest to somewhat flavourless dishes. The emphasis of flavour can be varied according to which herb predominates. Some receipes call for a little grated lemon peel which I found rather beguiling served with rabbit pie.

OYSTER SAUSAGES (MRS DAVIES)

"1lb veal scraped & pounded fine 1lb veal suet—1 pint of oysters dried in a Cloth—pound all well together— season with pepper, salt & Mace—add two eggs—stiffen with bread Crumbs—roll them up—& fry in boiling Lard—Excellent."

MS Receipt Book, Catherine Dixon, circa 1811. *Loaned by Miss Aldred.*

This receipt of course stems from the days of oysters at 6 a 1d. For today's cook, I suggest American canned oysters, or even clams. Do not be daunted by the combination of fish and flesh—the Chinese discovered this harmony a millennium ago. The sausages look better coated with breadcrumbs, and a dash of Soy in the mixture gives it zest. You will obtain a smooth compound with a blender.

A VENISON PASTY

"Get a neck and breast of venison, bone it, season it with pepper and salt according to your palate. Cut the breast into two or three pieces; but don't cut the fat off the neck if you can help it. Lay in the breast and neck-end first, and the best end of the neck on the top, that the fat may be whole; make a good rich puff-paste crust, let it be very thick on the sides, a good bottom crust, and a thick top. Cover the dish, then lay in your venison, put in half a pound of butter, about a quarter of a pint of water, close your pasty, and let it be baked two hours in a very quick oven. In the mean time, set on the bones of the venison in two quarts of water, with two or three blades of mace, an onion, a little piece of crust baked crisp and brown, a little whole pepper, cover it close, and let it boil softly over a slow fire, till about half is wasted, then strain it off. When the pasty comes out of the oven, lift up the lid and pour in the gravy.

"If your venison is not fat enough, take the fat of a loin of mutton, steep'd in a little rape vinegar and red wine twenty-four hours, then lay it on the top of the venison, and close your pasty. It is a wrong notion of some people, to think venison cannot be baked enough, and will first bake it in a false crust, and then bake it in the pasty; by this time the fine flavour of the venison is gone. No, if you want it to be very tender, wash it in warm milk and water, dry it in clean cloths till it is very dry; then rub it all over with vinegar, and hang it in the air. Keep it as long as you think proper, it will keep thus for a fortnight good; but be sure there be no moistness about it; if there is, you must dry it well, and throw ginger over it, and it will keep a long time. When you use it, just dip it in luke-warm water, and dry it. Bake it in a quick oven; if it is a large pasty, it will take three hours; then your venison will be tender, and have all the fine flavour. The shoulder makes a pretty pasty boned, and made as above with the mutton fat.

"A loin of mutton makes a fine pasty: take a large fat loin of mutton, let it hang four or five days, then bone it, leaving the meat as whole as you can; lay the meat twenty-four hours in red wine, and half a pint of rape vinegar; then take it out of the pickle, and order it as you do a pasty, and boil the bones in the same manner to fill the pasty, when it comes out of the oven."

The London Cook, or the Whole Art of Cookery Made Easy and Familiar, by William Gelleroy, Late Cook to her Grace the Dutchess of Argyle. And now to the Right Hon Sir Samuel Fludyer Bart, Lord Mayor of the City of London, 1762.

The fashion of treating mutton or even lamb to taste like venison enjoyed considerable popularity right up to the mid-nineteenth century, and the instructions for preparing the marinade were many and varied.

Coincident with the reappearance of venison in many butchers' shops today, I have noticed recently several recipes in the press for treating lamb thus. For those with a taste for game it is worth trying on a small leg, just plain roast. Her Grace of Argyll would doubtless have approved it.

VENISON SEMEY

"Make some paste with the crumb of a brown loaf grated very fine, a pint of white wine, two pounds of sugar, and the rind of an orange shred small, add a little nutmeg and salt; mix it well with the hand; roll it out; wrap the venison completely in this paste, and bake it for an hour. Serve it with white wine, boiled up with sugar, and spice; strew powder sugar over it."

The Cook's Dictionary and Housekeeper's Directory: A New Family Manual of Cookery and Confectionery, on A Plan of Ready Reference Never Hitherto attempted. By Richard Dolby, Late Cook at the Thatched House Tavern, St James's Street. 1st edition 1830.

———————————

It would appear from the quantities that this was intended to cover a complete haunch of venison! For those like myself with a predilection for venison and an attenuated purse, I would suggest applying this to a venison steak of, say, a pound weight. Use as much breadcrumb, wine, grated orange peel and a *little* sugar (two pounds!!) as will serve to cover it, bind it with beaten egg, and bake for ½ hour. Unlike Mr Dolby's patrons at The Thatched House Tavern, I hardly think we should care for his serving instructions. Use Cumberland sauce, or plain red currant jelly to accompany.

HOW TO ROAST TRIPE

"Cut it into oblong pieces; make a forced-meat of bread-crumbs, nutmeg, salt, pepper, lemon-peel, sweet herbs, and the yolks of eggs mixed all together, spread it on the fat side of half your tripe, and lay the other fat side next it;

then roll it lightly, and tie it with packthread; spit it, roast it, and baste it with butter; when it is enough lay it in your dish and make your sauce as follows. Melt some butter, and add to it what drops from the tripe, with mustard and lemon-juice. Boil it together and let your garnish be raspings."

The London Cook, or the Whole Art of Cookery Made Easy and Familiar, by William Gelleroy, Late Cook to her Grace the Dutchess of Argyle. And now to the Right Hon Sir Samuel Fludyer Bart, Lord Mayor of the City of London, 1762.

I hope this will prove a novel dish for tripe-enthusiasts to add to the many (and international) methods of tripe cookery. To the less enlightened cook, the plebeian tripe-and-onions, though in itself a fair dish, is often the only method of preparation used in this country. Our forebears knew better. When following the above receipt remember that by the instruction 'melt some butter' is meant to prepare a white *roux* (see 'Melted' Butter, p 155). The 'raspings' I have interpreted as fried breadcrumbs.

ROASTED TRIPE (*Another Way*)

"Take four pounds of double of fat tripe and putting some light forcemeat between the fat, roll it round and tie bards of fat bacon and some writing paper over it. Roast gently for an hour and a half: on serving take off the paper and bacon and pour over some white onion sauce."

The Art of Cookery Made Easy and Refined. By John Mollard, Cook; one of the Proprietors of the Freemasons' Tavern, Great Queen Street, Lincoln's Inn Fields. London 1801.

You will require a fairly rich forcemeat for this. I used butchers' pork sausage-meat lightened with breadcrumbs and enlivened with parsley and chopped onion. Fortunately today we need no longer resort to writing-paper, but wrap it in foil and seal both ends. Any type of tripe will serve, and in fact 'honeycomb' holds the forcemeat well.

TRIPE *at the* '*Jolly Sandboys*'

An early nineteenth-century stew from Dickens's *Old Curiosity Shop.* After reading the original, what amateur cook could forbear to try his hand at this? I quote:

" 'It's a stew of tripe' said the landlord, smacking his lips, 'and cowheel', smacking them again, 'and bacon' smacking them once more, 'and steak', smacking them for the fourth time, 'and peas, cauliflowers, new potatoes, and sparrowgrass, all working up together in one delicious gravy.' Having come to the climax, he smacked his lips a great many times, and taking a long hearty sniff of the fragrance that was hovering about, put on the cover again with the air of one whose toils on earth were over.

" 'At what time will it be ready?' asked Mr Codlin faintly. 'It'll be done to a turn', said the landlord, looking up at the clock, 'at twenty-two minutes before eleven.'

" 'Then,' said Mr Codlin, 'fetch me a pint of warm ale, and don't let nobody bring into the room even so much as a biscuit till the time arrives.' "

In my own experiment with this unctuous mixture I added 1 onion cut in slices, substituted old potato for new, used canned asparagus and frozen peas, and threw in a glass of claret, which I don't think the landlord would have found fault with. I used shin of beef, and the 'delicious gravy' I had prepared previously from **veal** bones, but doubtless any good stock would suffice. I presumed, and I think correctly, that this should be cooked in a casserole in the oven, at the lowest possible temperature, for 4 hours.

LAMB'S SWEETBREADS with Tops of Asparagus

"Blanch your sweetbreads, and put into cold water awhile, put them into a stewpan with a ladle of Broth, with pepper, salt, a small bunch of green onions and parsley, and a blade of Mace, stir in a bit of butter with flour, and stew all about half an hour; make ready a liaison of two or three eggs and cream, with a little minced parsley and nutmeg; put in your points of Asparagus (that I suppose to be boiled), and pour in your liaison, and take care it don't curdle; add some juice of lemon or orange and send it to table. You may make use of pease, young gooseberries or kidney beans for this, and all make a pretty Dish."

A Complete System of Cookery, 1759. *By William Verrall, Master of the White-Hart Inn in Lewes, Sussex.*
   This hostelry (still flourishing) had been since the fourteenth century the country seat of the Pelham family who held the Dukedom of Newcastle. Early in the eighteenth century they built Newcastle House on the other side of the High Street, and leased the former house to William Verrall's father as an inn. The book acknowledges receipts William Verrall collected from several years' experience 'under the celebrated Monsieur de St Clouet, Cook to His Grace the Duke of Newcastle'.

Canned asparagus will serve very well. I tried the 'young gooseberries'—excellent and unusual. Obviously you will use a double-boiler or *bain marie* for the liaison, which must not boil. The amateur cook who has attempted Sauce Hollandaise will know what I mean. Stir gently, or the asparagus will break up.

TO MAKE BRAIN CAKES

"When the head is cloven, take out the brains and clear them of any strings that may be amongst them. Cast them well with a knife, and mix them with the yolks of two raw eggs, a few crumbs of bread, parsley, pepper and salt, a spoonful and a half of flour, and the same quantity of cream; when they are very smooth, drop them with a spoon of the size of a small sugar biscuit, and fry them a light brown.

"Brain cakes make a very handsome corner dish, garnished with sliced orange."

The Practice of Cookery, Pastry, Confectionary, Pickling, Preserving etc, 1795. Mrs Frazer.

This is an interesting improvement on the usual fried brains and bacon. Treat the brains in the usual way (ie scald them, and when cold remove the blood vessels), chop them up as instructed and put them in a mixing bowl with all the additives and beat smooth. Fry them in butter, turning once, and garnish preferably with lemon and a few capers.

TO MAKE MINCHED PIES

"Take a large Neats Tongue shred it very small a pound and a halfe of Suet very well shred, Currans 3 pounds, halfe an ounce of beaten cloves and mace Season it with Salt. When you think it is fit halfe a preserved Orange or

instead of it a Pill. A quarter of a pound of Sugar a little
Lemmon Pill sliced very thin, put all these together, put
to it 3 spoonfull of verjuice and a quarter of a pint of
Sack."

MS Family Cookery Book, circa 1713, *Catherine Richardson. Loaned
by Mrs. Bowering.*

I was given an almost identical dish recently at the house of a
friend in Upton-upon-Severn, Worcestershire, *as a main course*. My
hostess told me she had it from her mother, who had it from her
great-great-grandmother. Apart from being unusual, it was excellent,
the ingredients being varied only in the use of pigs' tongues (previously
cooked) and for the 'verjuice' she used sherry. She notes also that the
addition of seedless raisins crept in during the twenties of this century,
but adds 'this is probably an improvement. Here is the receipt as I
had it.'

MRS MITCHELLS MINCEMEAT—Circa 1840

"Ingredients and Quantities for a reasonable bottling:
2lbs of stoned Whole Raisins, 1lb Sultanas, 1lb Currants,
8oz Chopped Candied Peel, Grated Rind from 1 Lemon
and One Orange, 1 well-boiled Lemon chopped Whole,
2 Pints of Minced Raw Apple, 2 Pigs Tongues, 2lb of
Fresh Beef Suet Chopped, ½ Teaspoon of Ground Ginger,
½ teaspoon of Cinnamon, 1 Teaspoon of Mace, 1 Teaspoon
of Salt, 1 Teaspoon of Allspice (All well ground) ½ Pint
of Brandy, ½ Pint of Medium Sherry.
Method:
Boil 1 Lemon one Hour (simmering). Chop finely using
all. Simmer Pigs Tongues until Tender (about ¾ hour)

Chop Finely. Mince Suet. Mince Apple. Mix all to-gether adding Brandy and Sherry Last. Fill Jars which MUST be Airtight. Top to cover with extra Brandy after packing down tightly. Allow to mature a minimum of Six Weeks. Will keep a year without deterioration after which it is still palatable but the flavours begin to coagulate.

"This Mince should be generously placed in a flaky Pastry 'top and bottom' Flat large Plate Pie. Serve with Brandy Butter and Brandy and bring to Table very Hot."

TO MAKE PEAR-PUDDINGS

"Take a cold Turky, Capon or cold Veal. Shred it very small; and put almost as much Beef-suet as your meat, and mince it very small. Then put Salt and Nutmeg grated, half a pound of Currants; a little grated-bread, and a little Flower. Then put in three yolks of Eggs, and one of the whites, beaten very well. Then take so much Cream, as will wet them, and make them up as big as a Bon-christian pear; and as you make them up, take a little flower in your hand, that they may not cling. Then put in little sticks at the bottom like the stems of Pears; or make them up in Balls. Butter the dish very well, and send them up in the same dish you bake them in. They will be baked in about half an hour: I think the dish needeth not to be covered, whiles it baketh. You may make minced Pyes thus; and bake them with Puff-past in a dish like a Florenden, and use Marrow instead of Suet."

The Closet of the Eminently Learned Sir Kenelm Digby, Kt, Opened. 1669.

Here is another solution to the problem of 'left-overs'. If you hardly fancy the currants, omit them unless you are making the 'minced Pyes'. The presentation as pears is interesting (particularly as he refers to a pear whose popular name and quality has not changed for three hundred years). The French use this device when making little 'picnic hams' they call *jambonneaux*. It occurs also in Hannah Glasse's *Pigeons au Poire*, qv.

COLLEGE PIE

"Soften as much vermicella as will thick line a basin well buttered then cover with a thin paste of short crust stick all the inside with slices of hard boiled egg then fill with beaf or pork seasoned, cover over with paste and bake it, after it is done have some Gravy jelly to pour in and let it remain in the dish till cold. E Barrow Kendal."

E. Keyworth's Receipt Book (MS), 1831. *Loaned by Miss Yolande Clements.*

One must assume the meat content of this strange confection to be minced, and if the 'gravy jelly' is stiffened with gelatine or aspic it will turn out of the basin when cold. I leave more adventurous souls than I to try this, but it might just be a good summer lunch, with salad.

SAVOURY MELANGE

"Take equal quantities of cold meat, (the greater variety the better) chop them small with an onion, pepper & salt mixed up in a good gravy and put into a mould with a little Vermicelli at the bottom of the Mould. Bake twenty

minutes serve up with a little brown gravy. For garnish
hard boiled eggs cut up or a little lemon peel. *Pentripant.*"

Amy Hull Receipt Book, MS. Loaned by Miss M. G. Hull.

This is evidently another version of the foregoing. It seems
popular enough in early Victorian households to merit a try.

TO STEW A HARE

"Pull your Hare to pieces, and bruise the Bones, and put it
into a Stew-pan, with three pints of strong Broth, and at
the same time put in an Onion, and a faggot of Sweet-
herbs; let it stew leisurely for four hours, then put in a
pint of Claret; let it stew two or three hours longer, 'till
'tis tender; take out what Bones you can find, with the
Herbs and Onion, if not dissolv'd; put in an Anchovy or
two with the Claret: Stewing so long, it will be thick
enough; you need only shake it up with half a pound of
Butter, when ready for the Table."

*A Collection of Above Three Hundred Receipts in Cookery, Physick and
Surgery; For the Use of all Good Wives, Tender Mothers, and Careful
Nurses. By several Hands. London, Printed for Richard Wilkin, at the
King's Head in St Paul's Church-yard. MDCCXIV.*

If you have already cut out and roasted the saddle, this is an
original way of dealing with the extremities for another meal. For the
fore and hind quarters I used 1 pint of stock, 2 good glasses of cooking
port or Tarragona (this gives a better flavour than claret), and followed the receipt thenceforth. Observe the instruction to cook very

slowly, ie the liquid should be just *tremblant*. The anchovies will dissolve, and the butter can be omitted. This will give you a rich, unctuous *purée*, to be consumed with spoons, and accompanied by red currant jelly.

FOR TO BAKE A HARE

"Take your Hare and perboyle him, and mince him, and then beat him in a mortar very fine, liver and all if you will, and season it with all kinde of spices and salte, and do him together with the yolkes of seven or eight egges, and when you have made him up together, drawe larde very thicke through him, and mingle them together, and put him into a Pye, and put in butter before you close him up."

The Good Huswifes Jewell, 1585. *By Thomas Dawson. Reprinted in 1620, entitled 'A Booke of Cookerie', and included a slimming recipe, probably worth trying, viz: 'To make one slender. Take Fennell and seethe it in Water, a very good quantity, and wringing out the Juyce thereof when it is sodde, drink it first and last, and it shall swage either man or woman.'*

I took the meat off the bone when it was reasonably tender and substituted a liquidiser for Dawson's mortar and pestle. By 'lard' he means bacon (cf the French term) which you can either draw through with a larding needle or put in layers of streaky rashers. With the addition of a glass of sherry or brandy this makes an excellent *pâté en croûte*, best eaten cold. For the spices I use coarse milled pepper, a pinch of mace and a few crushed juniper berries. Glaze the pastry with egg and bake in a hot (425°) oven for 15 minutes, then lower the heat to 300°, cover with foil or grease-proof, and bake for an hour.

PIGEONS

From the Middle Ages up to the end of the eighteenth century the pigeon was a staple and popular article of diet and, possibly because of its prolific breeding habit, reared for the table in most country houses. Many of these dovecotes, some of alarming magnitude, can still be seen, though housing, if anything at all, only ornamental fantails and pouters. They were mentioned regularly in the Star Chamber Accounts as being of two categories; the house-pigeon (from the dovecotes) and the wild variety, or wood-pigeon. Townspeople were prepared to pay 13 shillings a dozen in 1635 and 14 shillings in 1639, which in comparative terms would roughly equate with today's price. As usual, the physicians added their weight to the desirability of eating them: 'Pygeons be easily dygested and are very holsome to them which are flemmatike or pure melancholy.' (*Elyot's Castel of Helth, published in London* 1539.) While not entirely subscribing to their view, the pigeon has not the popularity it deserves, and if you can no longer find 'squabs'—the specially bred variety popular in France—the ordinary variety will serve well enough.

'. . . some pigeons, Davy, a couple of short-legged hens, a joint of mutton, and any pretty little tiny kickshaws, tell William cook . . .': William Shakespeare, 1564. From *Henry IV*, Part 2, v, i.

Here are some of the ways our forefathers sent them to the table.

PIGEONS IN PIMLICO

"Take the livers, with some fat and lean of ham or bacon, mushrooms, truffles, parsley, and sweet herbs; season with beaten mace, pepper, and salt; beat all these together with two raw eggs, put it into the bellies, roll them all in a thin slice of veal, over that a thin slice of bacon; wrap them up in white paper, spit them on a small spit, and roast them. In

86

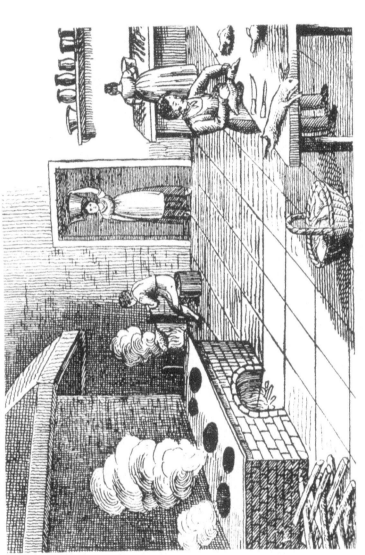

Page 87   *Preparation for dinner circa 1800. Note the turnspit and oven for food-warming*

Page 88 *A seventeenth-century 'kitchen-dining room'. Roasting, boiling and baking are simultaneously in action, probably at an inn*

the mean time make for them a ragoo of truffles and mushrooms chopped small, with parsley cut small; put to it half a pint of good veal gravy, thicken with a piece of butter rolled in flour; an hour will do your pigeons; baste them, when enough lay them in your dish, take off the paper, and pour your sauce over them. Garnish with patties, made thus: take veal and cold ham, beef-suet, an equal quantity, some mushrooms, sweet herbs, and spice; chop them small, set them on the fire, and moisten with milk or cream; then make a little puff-paste, roll it, and make little patties about an inch deep and two inches long; fill them with the above ingredients, cover them close and bake them; lay six of them round a dish. This makes a fine dish for a first course."

The Art of Cookery Made Plain & Easy, which far excels any Thing of the Kind yet published, London 1747. *By Mrs Glasse.*

My researches have failed to reveal where this odd name originated, but it had certainly nothing to do with the formerly fashionable quarter of London (now once again domiciling the *haut monde*). Mrs Glasse's instructions will appear a trifle daunting to the amateur cook —as indeed they did to me when I essayed this dish. However, as in so many eighteenth-century receipts, I felt it permissible to bend the rules to the point where a reasonable approximation of the dish can be achieved without an army of scullions and spit-turners, and still feel the result could be served without embarrassment to the select company of be-wigged guests before whom it was originally placed. Here is how I went about it. For 4 pigeons:

Take ¼lb of chicken-livers, firmed in a little butter, chopped up with 3 or 4 rashers of streaky bacon, a few mushrooms, parsley and seasoning, using 2 anchovy fillets for salt (see: 'To Make Force-Meat for Pigeons, p 91). Stiffen the mixture with breadcrumbs and beaten egg and stuff the birds, having tied the breasts with bacon. Wrap them in foil with a knob of butter, and roast in the oven at 350° for 35–40 minutes according to size. The 'ragoo' will not, of course, incorporate truffles, but is otherwise simple. If you decide to be grand and serve the garnish, you can cut corners by buying your small *vol-au-vent* cases from the baker, fill them with chopped mushroom and crisped bacon (or your favourite filling) previously heated in a creamy white sauce, and gently warmed in the oven.

TO STEW PIGEONS

"Season your pigeons with pepper and salt, a few cloves and mace, and some sweet herbs; wrap this seasoning up in a piece of butter, and put it in their bellies; then tie up the neck and vent, and half roast them: put them in a stew-pan, with a quart of good gravy, a little white wine, a few pepper-corns, three or four blades of mace, a bit of lemon, a bunch of sweet herbs, and a small onion; stew them gently till they are enough; then take the pigeons out, and strain the liquor through a sieve; skim it, and thicken it in your stew-pan; put in the pigeons, with some pickled mushrooms and oysters, stew it five minutes, and put the pigeons in a dish, and the sauce over."

The Art of Cookery Made Plain & Easy, which far excels any Thing of the Kind yet published, London 1747. *By Mrs Glasse.*

This is quite simple and self-explanatory, save that I prefer red wine (2 glasses) and a dozen or so small pickling onions. I used lemon *peel* (small piece) and omitted the refinement of mushrooms and oysters. Cook in a covered casserole in a slow oven for 2 hours.

TO MAKE FORCE-MEAT FOR PIGEONS

"Take a little fat bacon, beat it in a marble mortar, take two anchovies, two or three of the pigeons' livers, chop them together; add a little lemon-peel shred, a little beaten mace, nutmeg, Cayenne, stale bread crumbs, and beef-suet an equal quantity, mix all together with an egg."

The Art of Cookery Made Plain & Easy, which far excels any Thing of the Kind yet published, London 1747. *By Mrs Glasse.*

PIGEONS AU POIRE*

"Make a good force-meat as above, cut the feet quite off, stuff them in the shape of a pear, roll them in the yolk of an egg and then in crumbs of bread, stick the leg at the top, and butter a dish to lay them in; then send them to an oven to bake, but do not let them touch each other; when they are enough, lay them in a dish, and pour in good gravy thickened with the yolk of an egg, or butter rolled in flour; do not pour your gravy over the pigeons, You may garnish with lemon. It is a pretty genteel dish: or, for change, lay one pigeon in the middle, the rest round, and stewed spinage between; poached eggs on the spinage. Garnish with notched lemon and orange cut into quarters, and have melted butter in boats.

"Or thus: bone your pigeons, and stuff them with force-meat; make them in the shape of a pear, with one foot stuck at the small end to appear like the stalk of a pear; rub them over with the yolk of an egg, and strew some crumbs

* A concession to the despised French!

91

bread on; fry them in a pan of good dripping a nice light brown; put them in a drainer to drain all the fat off; then put them in a stew-pan with a pint of gravy, a gill of white wine, an onion stuck with cloves; cover them close and stew them for half an hour; take them out, skim off all the fat, and take out the onion; put in some butter rolled in flour, a spoonful of catchup, the same of browning, some truffles and morels, pickled mushrooms, two artichoke-bottoms cut in six pieces each, a little salt and Cayenne pepper, the juice of half a lemon; stew it five minutes, put in your pigeons and make them hot; put them in your dish and pour the sauce over them. Garnish with fried force-meat balls, or with a lemon cut in quarters."

The Art of Cookery Made Plain & Easy, which far excels any Thing of the Kind yet published, London 1747. *By Mrs Glasse.*

If you have a satisfactory relationship with your poulterer, ask him to bone the pigeons for you. As these birds have no fat put fat bacon in your stuffing, and tie the vent (with the leg protruding) with thread to preserve the pear-shape. Observe that 'melted butter' in the eighteenth-century kitchen meant a creamy white sauce. (See 'Melted Butter', p 155.)

PIGEONS TRANSMOGRIFIED

"Take your pigeons, season them with pepper and salt, take a large piece of butter, make a puff-paste, and roll each pigeon in a piece of paste; tie them in a cloth so that the paste do not break, boil them in a good deal of water; they will take an hour and a half boiling; untie them carefully that they do not break; lay them in the dish, and you may pour a little good gravy in the dish. They will eat exceeding good and nice, and will yield sauce enough of a very agreeable relish."

The Art of Cookery Made Plain & Easy, which far excels any Thing of the Kind yet published, London 1747. *By Mrs Glasse.*

You will note that Mrs Glasse, like myself, was rather apprehensive about the crust breaking. I think she meant each bird to be tied separately, in its own cloth, and this is what I did. Further, to make it more compact in its envelope of puff-paste, I removed the legs entirely and added them to the constitution of the 'good gravy' she advises. Red currant jelly goes well with this dish.

PIGEONS COMPOTE

"Take six young pigeons and skewer them as for boiling; make a force-meat thus: grate the crumb of a penny loaf, half a pound of fat bacon, shred some sweet herbs and parsley fine, two shalots, or a little onion, a little lemon-peel, a little grated nutmeg, season it with pepper and salt, and mix it up with the yolk of two eggs; put it into the craws and bellies, lard them down the breast, and fry them brown with a little butter; then put them in a stew-pan, with a pint of strong brown gravy, a gill of white wine; stew them three quarters of an hour, thicken it with a little butter rolled in flour, season with salt and Cayenne pepper, put the pigeons in the dish, and strain the gravy over them. Lay some hot force-meat balls round them, and send them up hot."

The Art of Cookery Made Plain & Easy, which far excels any Thing of the Kind yet published, London 1747. *By Mrs Glasse.*

If you do not want the trouble of larding, tie the breasts with rashers of streaky bacon after frying them. On p 191 is another forcemeat incorporating the livers, but as these are small and sometimes have a broken gall, use two or three chicken livers.

PIGEON PIE

"Take 4 Young Pigeons nicely picked and washed season them well with pepper and salt, cayenne pepper and a little mace; mix a little Butter and Flour with a little of the seasoning, and put it inside of each Pigeon place them in the Dish with the breasts downwards and put the Pinions and Gizzards in the middle—Add the yolks of 5 Eggs boiled hard, and a little Flour and butter mixed; then put as much Beef or Mutton Gravy as you think necessary and cover it with good Puff paste—a slice of veal at the bottom of the Dish improves it much—Lady Chichester."

Elizabeth Evans, Walthamstow MS Receipt Book. Loaned by Mrs Philippa Gregory.

Leave out the gizzards, which are inclined to be tough, and substitute 4 chicken livers well washed and cleaned. Despite Lady Chichester's instruction, I used whole hard-boiled eggs and added a glass of cooking claret to the gravy.

Eliza Acton (1845) in a similar receipt adds: 'It is a great improvement to fill the birds with small mushroom-buttons'—and it is.

TO ROST FINE MEAT

"When the Capon, Chickens, or Fowl, have been long enough before the fire, to be through hot, and that it is time to begin to baste them: baste them once all over very well with fresh Butter; then presently powder it all over very thin with Flower. This by continuing turning before the fire, will make a thin crust, which will keep in all the juyce of the meat. Therefore baste no more, nor do any thing to it, till the meat be enough rosted. Then baste it well with Butter as before, which will make the crust relent and fall away; which being done, and that the meat is growing brown on the Out-side, besprinkle it over with a little ordinary white Salt in gross-grains; and continue turning, till the outside be brown enough.

"The Queen useth to baste such meat with yolks of fresh Eggs beaten thin, which continue to do all the while it is roasting."

The Closet of the Eminently Learned Sir Kenelm Digby, Kt, Opened. 1669.

This method is an improvement on the usual modern buttered-paper when cooking in the oven, and of course ideal for (electric) spit-roasting. Follow his direction to use *gros-sel*, and not 'kitchen' salt.

Despite the name-drop, the Queen's usage seems too extravagant with eggs, and rather messy in the dripping-pan.

TO MAKE A CAPARATA

"Cut down a cold fowl, and take all the skin and fat off it, except the rump; mince all the meat very small with a knife; break the bones, and put them on with some water, lemon-peel, and a blade of mace; let them boil until all the substance is out of them; strain it off, and thicken it with a little butter knead in flour; chop some yolks of hard eggs; put the minced fowl and eggs into the sauce; let it get two or three boils. Just before dishing, put in the squeeze of a lemon, a scrape of nutmeg, and a proper quantity of salt; broil the back of the fowl, and lay it on the top of the caparata. A cold roasted turkey may be done in the same manner."

The Practice of Cookery, Pastry, Confectionary, Pickling, Preserving etc, 1795. *By Mrs Frazer.*

In today's kitchen this strangely titled confection might be listed under 'left-overs'.

Confronted with the considerable remains of a large boiling fowl (used originally to make a small risotto) I kept the parson's nose on the carcase as instructed, and passed the skinned and defatted remains through the coarse mincer, having put aside the bones. These last I boiled up in a good pint of water, adding a chicken-stock cube to the spice and lemon peel. Reducing it by half, I strained and thickened it, put in the minced fowl and eggs, and simmered it slowly to heat well through. The back, on which I had retained the skin, I brushed with oil and browned under the grill to form a 'lid' for the dish. This I awarded to myself, as chef's perquisites because I have a liking for chicken skin, the 'oyster' and the parson's nose.

I can understand that this method could well be applied to the perennial problem of left-over Christmas turkey.

TO MARINATE CHICKENS

"Take chickens, quarter them, and lay them for two or three hours to marinate in vinegar or verjuice, and juice of lemon, salt, pepper, cloves, and bay-leaves; then make a batter with flour, white-wine or water, the yolks of eggs, salt, and melted butter; beat all these well together, drain your chickens, and dry them with a cloth, dip them into it, and broil them; and when they are well coloured, dish them up in the form of a pyramid, and serve them up with fry'd parsley and slices of lemon. Garnish with lemon, and have gravy in basons.

"We sometimes drudge them with flour instead of dipping them in batter."

The London Cook, or the Whole Art of Cookery Made Easy and Familiar, by William Gelleroy, Late Cook to her Grace the Dutchess of Argyle. And now to the Right Hon Sir Samuel Fludyer Bart, Lord Mayor of the City of London, 1762.

———————

Here is one way of inducting some flavour into those mass-produced broilers and poussins which everyone rightly declares to taste of cotton-wool. Use wine or cider vinegar and whole peppercorns.

TO BUTTER CHICKEN

"First boyl them, then cut them up in Joynts and skin them, put them into a Stew Pan with half a Pint of thick raw Cream, some broken white Pepper in a piece of Muslin, 4 or 5 Cloves of Shallot, stew it till tis hot, then put it into a Quarter of a Pound of Butter shaking it well, just as you take it up put in some boyl'd Parsley, shred very small and after its off the fire put in the Juice of a Lemon."

MS Recipe—Mrs Cholwich. From Dorset Dishes of the 17th Century (published 1967) by J. Stevens Cox, FSA, being a selection from two family manuscript sources in the possession of G. Stevens Cox.

This receipt is taken from a folio MS of the Bragge family of Beaminster and Sadborrow, and attributed to various friends who gave them to the Bragge household between the years 1660 and 1680.

I used a boiling fowl, simmered very slowly until tender in the usual way (with a mirepoix of carrot, onion, bayleaf etc). A ½ pint of single cream will serve, as it will thicken with cooking. The end result somewhat resembles the modern *chicken sauce suprême*, but is better for being finished in the cream and butter. I serve it with rice cooked in the chicken stock, with a few mushrooms for garnish.

A DUNELM OF COLD FOWL

"Stew a few small mushrooms in their own liquor and a bit of butter, a quarter of an hour; mince them very small and add them with their liquor to the minced fowl, with also a little pepper and salt, some cream, and a bit of butter rubbed in less than half a teaspoonful of flour. Simmer three or four minutes and serve on thin sippets of bread."

A New System of Domestic Cookery formed upon Principles of Economy, and adapted to the Use of Private Families, 1807. By Mrs Maria

Eliza Rundle. (Mrs Maria Eliza Rundle (1745–1828) produced in this book a rival to Mrs Glasse in popularity; the 65th edition was published in 1841 and, in an amended form, appeared as late as 1893.)

This appears to be the original receipt on which is based that old American favourite 'Chicken (or Turkey) à la King'. As it stands, it is a trifle dull, and might almost be listed under 'sick-room' or 'invalid' cookery. As a speedy supper dish with left-overs, try adding a little paprika, or curry powder; or diced green peppers, or a little lemon juice, or garlic powder and chopped parsley. It will need rather longer to get thoroughly hot. Serve on toast.

A SAVOURY AND NOURISHING BOILED CAPON DEL CONTE DI TRINO, A MILANO

"Take a fat and fleshy Capon, or a like Hen; Dress it in the ordinary manner, and cleanse it within from the guts, &c. Then put in the fat again into the belly, and split the bones of the legs and wings (as far as you may, not to deface the fowl) so as the Marrow may distil out of them. Add a little fresh Butter and Marrow to it; season it with Salt, Pepper, and, what other Spice you like, as also savoury herbs. Put the Capon with all these condiments into a large strong sound bladder of an Ox (first well washed and scoured with Red-wine) and tie it very close and fast to the top, that nothing may ouse out, nor any water get in (and there must be void space in the bladder, that the flesh may have room to swell and ferment in; therefore it must be a large one). Put this to boil for a couple of hours in a Kettle of water, or till you find by touching the Bladder, that the Capon is tender and boiled enough. Then serve it up in a dish, in the Bladder (dry wiped) which when you cut, you will find a precious and nourishing liquor to eat with bread, and the Capon will be short, tender, most savoury and full of juyce, and very nourishing.

"I conceive, that if you put enough Ox-marrow, you need no butter; and that it may do well to add Amber-greece, Dates-sliced and pithed, Raisins, Currants, and a little Sugar.

"Peradventure this might be done well in a Silver-flagon close luted, set in *Balneo bulliente*, as I make the nourishing broth or gelly of Mutton or Chicken, &c."

The Closet of the Eminently Learned Sir Kenelm Digby, Kt, Opened. 1669.

———————

Although strictly speaking this method of dealing with a boiling fowl was the result of Sir Kenelm's travels abroad, and therefore hardly traditional English, I have nevertheless included it as probably typical in a Restoration household, especially since contemporary diarists, including Samuel Pepys, frequently refer to 'boyl'd chickens' at their dinner parties.

The reader will probably share my amusement in this writer's insistence on what we term 'name-dropping'. Almost every receipt in this not inconsiderable book bears testimony to his distinguished circle of friends at court and elsewhere.

Unlike the Count di Trino, we are unable to provide ox bladders at will, and I substituted an envelope of aluminium cooking-foil, in which I included a lump of butter. To obtain the marrow from the legs, scald them in boiling water for a few minutes, when the scales will come off easily, and the legs split with a sharp knife. Simmer very slowly in a large saucepan for $2\frac{1}{2}$ to 3 hours, and unwrap on the hot serving dish. You can doubtless achieve the same result if your fowl is boiled in those treated plastic envelopes sold as 'Roastabags'. Forget the 'ambergreece' etc, unless you are a purist. Their inclusion was treated only as a conception by the author.

The second method he suggests is what we would term 'jugging', or setting one sealed vessel inside another to cook slowly, as in a double-boiler or, since we now favour French terms rather than Latin, a *bain-marie*. What is also interesting is the recent revival of this method of cooking in an oblong, lidded vessel of unglazed earthenware sold as a 'Roman' chicken-pot, to be found in the best department stores.

TO MUMBLE RABBITS AND CHICKENS

"Put into the bellies of your rabbits, or chickens, some parsley, an onion, and the liver; set it over the fire in the stew-pan with as much water mixed with a little salt as will cover them; when they are half boiled take them out, and shred the parsley, liver, and onion; tear the flesh from the bones of the rabbit in small flakes, and put it into the stew-pan again with a very little of the liquor it was boiled in, a pint of white wine, some gravy, half a pound or more of butter, and some grated nutmeg; when 'tis enough, shake in a little flour, and thicken it up with butter. Serve it on sippets."

The Compleat Housewife or Accomplish'd Gentlewoman's Companion, 15th edition, 1753. By Eliza Smith.

———————

'When 'tis enough' seems a little vague. I tried this in a casserole, on a slow flame on top of the oven for about an hour. The wine will reduce considerably; ½lb of butter is too much. Try 4oz, and when adding flour to thicken, boil up and then add more butter if necessary. The sippets, or squares of toast, are optional, but an improvement on general presentation.

Vegetables

TO MAKE FRITTERS OF SPINNEDGE

"Take a good deale of Spinnedge, and washe it cleane, then boyle it in faire water, and when it is boyled, then take it forth and let the water runne from it, then chop it with the backe of a knife, and then put in some egges and grated Bread, and season it with sugar, sinamon, ginger, and pepper, dates minced fine, and currans, and rowle them like a ball, and dippe them in Batter made of Ale and flower."

The Good Huswifes Jewell 1585. Wherein is to be found most excellent and rare Devises for conceites in Cookery, found out by the practise of Thomas Dawson. 1596.

This is a quite simple dish which can serve either as a vegetable, or if you dare, as a sweet.

Take spinach (½lb per person will be enough) and put it on to boil in the ordinary way ie with *very* little water and a knob of butter. When cooked through, drain it and chop it very fine. In a bowl beat up 2 eggs and 6 to 8oz of breadcrumbs, add the chopped spinach, salt and pepper, a small pinch of ginger and cinnamon, and mix well. Form into small balls (or rissoles), dip in the batter and fry in deep fat. Add currants and dates and you have an unusual sweet, over which I recommend you pour cream.

TO STEW CUCUMBERS (1)

"Take about a dozen of large Cucumbers, and slice them; then take three Onions and cut them very small; put these in a Saucepan over the Fire to stew, with a little salt, stir them often, till they are tender, and then drain them in a Cullender as dry as possible; then flour them, and put some Pepper to them, and fry them in Butter till they are brown, and put to them a Glass of Clarret, and when this is mix'd with them, serve them under Roast Mutton, or Lamb, or else serve them on a Plate upon Fryd Sippets."

The Housekeeper's Pocket Book and Compleat family Cook. Containing above Three Hundred Curious and Uncommon Receipts. With Plain and Easy Instructions for preparing and dressing everything suitable for an Elegant Entertainment. By Mrs Sarah Harrison of Devonshire; London 1733 (and a further nine editions).

Once again the old writers used the term 'stew' for a different method of cooking. The odd mixture of cucumber with onion was, and rightly, considered quite admissible. (Curry devotees will re-collect the combination of these in a cucumber *sambal*).

Two large cucumbers peeled and sliced and one medium-sized onion chopped fine are sufficient. Put them over very moderate heat so that they cook in their own juices. Then follow the directions given.

TO STEW CUCUMBERS (2)

"Pare some large cucumbers, and slice them about the thickness of half a crown; spread them on a clean coarse cloth, to drain the water from them; pare and slice some large onions roundways; flour the cucumbers, and fry them and the onions in browned butter; when you see them brown, take them up carefully from the butter. Then take a clean pan, and put three or four spoonfuls of warm water in it; put in a quarter of a pound of fresh butter rolled in flour; stir it on the fire until it is melted; mix in a teaspoonful of the flour of mustard; put in the cucumbers, and season it with salt and spices; cover up the pan, and let them stew about a quarter of an hour, softly shaking the pan, and dish them up."

The Practice of Cookery, Pastry, Confectionary, Pickling, Preserving etc, 1795. By Mrs Frazer. Loaned by Mrs Rosemary Waterhouse.

Written sixty years later, this alternative method approximates more closely to what we mean by 'stew', and is in fact a good vegetable dish to accompany any meat. The *tour de main* lies in the addition of mustard, which counteracts the otherwise bland flavour.

CUCUMBERS WITH EGGS

"Pare, quarter, and cut six large cucumbers into squares, about the size of a dice. Put them into boiling water, and give them a boil. Then take them out of the water, and put them into a stew-pan, with an onion stuck with cloves, a slice of ham, a quarter of a pound of butter, and a little salt.

Page 105 *Open fireplace at the Old Castle Inn, Old Sarum, Wilts, showing bread-oven at left*

Page 106   *The great kitchen of the Prince Regent's Pavilion at Brighton, showing spits and bottle-jacks*

Set it over the fire a quarter of an hour, keep it close covered, skim it well, and shake it often, for it is apt to burn. Then dredge in a little flour, and put in as much veal gravy as will just cover the cucumbers. Stir it well together, and keep a gentle fire under it till no scum will rise. Then take out the ham and onion, and put in the yolks of two eggs beat up with a tea-cupful of good cream. Stir it well for a minute, then take it off the fire, and just before you put it into the dish, squeeze in a little lemon-juice. Lay on the top of it five or six poached eggs."

The London Art of Cookery, and Housekeeper's Complete Assistant. On a New Plan. Made Plain and Easy to the Understanding of every Housekeeper, Cook, and Servant in the Kingdom. By John Farley, Principal Cook at the London Tavern. Original edition 1783, *reprinted* 12 *times, last edition* 1811.

TO DRESS PARSNIPS

"Scrape well three or four large roots, cleansing well their outside, and cutting off as much of the little end as is Fibrous, and of the great end as is Hard. Put them into a possnet or pot, with about a quart of Milk upon them, or as much as will cover them in boiling, which do moderately till you find they are tender. This may be in an hour and a half, sooner or later, as the roots are of a good kind. Then take them out, and scrape all the outside into a pulpe, like the pulpe of roasted apples which put in a dish upon a chafing dish of Coals, with a little of the Milk you boiled them in, put to them; not so much as to drown them, but only to imbibe them: and then with stewing, the pulpe will imbibe all that milk. When you see it is drunk in, put

G

to the Pulpe a little more of the same Milk, and stew that, till it be drunk in. Continue doing this till it hath drunk in a good quantity of the Milk, and is well swelled with it, and will take no more, which may be in a good half hour. Eat them so, without Sugar or Butter, for they will have a natural sweetness, that is beyond Sugar, and will be Unctuous, so as not to need Butter."

The Closet of the Eminently Learned Sir Kenelm Digby, Kt, Opened. 1669.

───────────

Sir Kenelm adds that parsnips cut 'into little pieces is the best food for tame Rabets, and makes them sweet'.

TO FRY POTATOES

"Cut your potatoes into thin slices, as large as a crown piece, fry them brown, lay them in a dish, pour melted butter, sack and sugar over them."

The Practice of Cookery, Pastry, Confectionary, Pickling, Preserving etc, 1795. By Mrs Frazer. Loaned by Mrs Rosemary Waterhouse.

───────────

I admit I approached this gastronomic curiosity with a certain trepidation, but secure in the knowledge that manufactured 'crisps' are now flavoured with everything from bacon to cheese, I tried it and found it good. Melted butter in this case means what it says, and I used a sweet sherry. It may at least prove a talking point at your next cocktail party.

POTATO FRITTERS

"A savoury Dish for Supper, Breakfast or Dinner. Skin and parboil some potatoes, and cut them into slices about as thick as a crown piece: beat up 2 eggs, mix with them about a table spoonful of fine bread crumbs, and the same quantity of finely chopped lean ham or tongue, seasoning it with a little salt and pepper. Into this mixture dip the slices of potato, and fry them in plenty of hot lard or good dripping, but let it be quite hot before they are put in; also let the slices of potato be well covered with the mixture, which, if not thick enough to adhere like a batter, should be made so with the addition of a few more bread crumbs. When done serve on a hot dish; but be careful to drain them well from fat by putting them into a collander or sieve, and keeping them before the fire till they are all done."

Emma Smith, Alvaston Hall, Derbyshire, November 1855, MS Loaned by Mrs Isabel Smith.

I would advise deep-frying these fritters (which are excellent) in a chip-basket, using any good cooking oil. Try them as an interesting alternative to chips with your fish, and substitute crumbled, crisped streaky bacon for the ham.

(FRIED) CELERY

"Cut off the green tops of six or eight heads of celery, and take off the outside stalks. Wash them well, and pare the roots clean. Then have ready half a pint of white wine, the yolks of three eggs beat fine, and a little salt and nutmeg. Mix all well together with flour into a batter, and dip every head into the batter, and fry them in butter. When they be enough, lay them in your dish, and pour melted butter over them."

The London Art of Cookery, and Housekeeper's Complete Assistant. On a New Plan. Made Plain and Easy to the Understanding of every Housekeeper, Cook, and Servant in the Kingdom. By John Farley, Principal Cook at the London Tavern. Original edition 1783, *reprinted* 12 *times, last edition* 1811.

A rather less haphazard batter which I used for this: 2oz butter; ¾ pint dry white wine and water mixed; a good pinch of salt and nutmeg; ¾lb flour; 2 eggs, well beaten. Pour on to the butter a fair gill of the wine/water mixture *boiling*. When dissolved add the rest *cold*. Into the lukewarm liquid mix by degrees and smoothly the flour and salt, then stir in the beaten eggs. The result is light, crisp batter As a hot 'starter' for dinner this is quick, easy, and presentable.

RADISHES AU BLOND

"Boil in some stock, and drain your radishes, then put them into a stewpan, with veal blond; simmer them for half an hour; add a little nutmeg and verjuice; stir them occasionally, and when the radishes are flavoured and well coloured, dish them, strew bread crumbs over, and brown it in the oven."

The Cook's Dictionary, and Housekeeper's Directory: A New Family Manual of Cookery and Confectionery, on A Plan of Ready Reference

Never Hitherto attempted. By Richard Dolby, Late Cook at The Thatched House Tavern, St James's Street. 1st edition 1830.

Veal blond presents some difficulty, and is more appropriate to the chef's kitchen. A more domestic approach would be any good meat stock flavoured with a few bacon rinds or a little ham and mushroom stalks. Reduce it a little and simmer the radishes as instructed. For 'verjuice' I used a teaspoonful of wine-vinegar. A vegetable sufficiently unusual to serve as a talking point at dinner. It goes well with lamb, having an affinity with the turnip. But omit mint sauce on this occasion.

BUBBLE AND SQUEAK, OR FRIED BEEF OR MUTTON AND CABBAGE

'When 'midst the frying Pan, in accents savage,
The Beef, so surly, quarrels with the Cabbage.'

"For this, as for a Hash, select those parts of the joint that have been least done:—it is generally made with slices of cold boiled salted Beef, sprinkled with a little Pepper, and just lightly browned with a bit of Butter in a frying-pan: *if it is fried too much it will be hard.*
    "Boil a Cabbage, squeeze it quite dry, and chop it small; take the Beef out of the frying-pan, and lay the Cabbage in it; sprinkle a little pepper and salt over it; keep the pan moving over the fire for a few minutes; lay the Cabbage in the middle of a dish, and the Meat round it."

Apicius Redevivus or The Cook's Oracle. By William Kitchiner, MD, 1817.

I include this traditional English dish, with its onomatopeoic title, largely to demonstrate the difference between what is served today under that name, viz mixed cold greens and potato, fried into a kind of cake, and the recipe whose origins are lost in the mists of time. Who has not been confronted with the remains of that other old English stand-by—boiled beef and carrots? Fry it preferably in oil.

TO STEW MUSHROOMS

"Take some strong broth, season it with a bunch of sweet herbs, some spice and anchovies, setting it over the fire till 'tis hot; then put in the mushrooms, and just let them boil up; then take the yolks of eggs, with a little minced thyme, parsley, and some grated nutmeg; and stir it over the fire till 'tis thick. Serve it up with sliced lemon."

The Compleat Housewife or Accomplish'd Gentlewoman's Companion, 15th edition, 1753. By Eliza Smith.

This revealed itself as a sort of scrambled egg with mushroom *de luxe*. A good light 'starter' for a dinner The yolks of 4 eggs to ½lb of button mushrooms seemed about right, with enough 'strong broth' for four people Serve in soup bowls or consommé cups.

A NOTE ON SALADS

These are rarely referred to specifically in old cookery books, the assumption being that their use was too common to describe. A small book on the subject by John Evelyn, the diarist, appeared in 1699 entitled *Acetaria. A Discourse of Sallets*, in which he gives a general definition of his subject.

'We are by Sallet to understand a particular composition of certain *Crude* and Fresh Herbs, such as usually are, or may safely be eaten with some *Acetaceous* Juice, *Oyl*, Salt etc. to give them Gust and Vehicle.'

The interesting word is 'safely', since the varying merits and demerits of herbs and vegetables was a popular subject of disputation among the old doctors and philosophers, and in the popular and widely-read Herbals of the time. Awful warnings were issued on the dangers of consuming certain vegetables, 'cabbage especially', says Burton in his *Anatomy of Melancholy* 'is disallowed. It causeth troublesome dreams and sends up black vapours to the brain . . . and heaviness to the soul'. Even earlier, in the sixteenth century, Dr Andrew Boorde was writing in his *Dyetary*: 'Our English nature cannot live by roots, by watery herbs or such beggary baggage.' But as the cultivation of gardens became more popular the old fears were forgotten and the salad became a regular article of diet, very much as we know it today.

There are, however, a few crumbs of knowledge to be gathered from Evelyn and other writers which are worth pursuing. *Globe artichokes*, for instance, 'with Oyl, vinegar, Salt and Pepper gratefully recommend a Glass of Wine, at the *end* of Meals'. Thus Dr Muffet, a court Physician in the sixteenth century. The writer adds, 'Tis not very long since this noble *Thistle* . . . [was] so rare in England that they were commonly sold for *Crowns* apiece.'

Of *Cucumbers*, Evelyn advises, 'Let them be pared and cut in thin slices with a clove or two of *Onion* to correct the Crudity.' The reader will see that this combination often appears in certain soups and prepared dishes, and is absolutely valid.

Of *Fennel*, he notes that 'the tender tufts emerging', ie the feathery leaf above the bulb, can be minced and eaten with oil, vinegar and pepper. (This is an interesting additive to potato salad.) And goes further to say of pepper what all should know but some do not, viz 'it should be grossly contused. When too minutely beaten (as oft we find it) to an impalpable dust,' he considered it 'very pernicious'.

Melons were often eaten in salads, a practice which is returning today and, an interesting departure for summer, the tops of *mint* with the juice of an orange and a little sugar.

Turnips were eaten in salads, recommended to be 'no bigger than a seedling radish'. (A hint for gardeners to utilise their 'thinnings'.)

Sage, 'the flowers only, in a cold Sallet, yet so as not to domineer'. (They look pretty, too.)

The use in salads of what we term herbs (a word the old writers often used to cover the entire vegetable kingdom) was widespread, but these scarcely come within the compass of cookery. Nasturtium seeds (green), marigold flowers, even small rosebuds were cast into the salad bowl for additional flavour and appearance. In Gervase Markham's *The English Hus-wife* (1615), which he declared to be 'A Worke very profitable and necessarie', there appears his instruction *To compound an excellent Sallat*, which involved the use of chopped almonds, raisins, figs, capers, olives, sage and spinach with a dressing of oil, vinegar and sugar. That done, peeled oranges and lemons were placed on top, to be covered with the thin leaf of red 'Colefloure', further covered with olives, pickled cucumbers and the heart of lettuce! Something here for the experimental cook, though I confess to not having tried it, deterred by the difficulty of assembling all the ingredients simultaneously!

Salad dressing often, as today, incorporated *Mustard*—'of the best Tewksberry'. (This can now be bought prepared, and is excellent.) Or, 'ground mustard-seed, winnowed, dried and tempered to a pap with vinegar in which the raspings of Horse radish have been steeped: then, cutting an Onion and putting it into a small earthen Gally-pot, or some thick Glass of that shape; pour the mustard over it and close with a cork'. A task for the home pickle-maker, or any kitchen alchemist. For another home-prepared mustard see p 170.

Sweets and Puddings

TO MAKE CREAM TOASTS

"Take 6 yolks of Eggs, a Quart of Cream, some Sugar and beaten Cinnamon and grated Lemon Peel and mix them all well together, then take some slices of french Bread a Quarter of an Inch thick, wash them and put them into the Cream to soak and when soak'd take them out and dip 'em in some Eggs only and fry them and serve them hot with Sugar and Orange."

Dorset Dishes of the 17th Century, collected by J. Stevens Cox, FSA, 1967. MS recipe from the Bragge family of Beaminster and Sadborrow.

This would seem to bear some relationship to the cinnamon toast of Edwardian tea-parties, but is a more elaborate version which I have used as a dessert (accompanied by a glass of Tokay, or one of the sweeter French white wines). The quantities are somewhat alarming and were doubtless intended for a large family. For 6 people I adjusted to 3 egg yolks and a ½-pint carton of single cream, a good flavouring of powdered cinnamon, and a little grated peel, sugar to taste, but don't make it too sweet. I used ordinary sliced bread

('French' bread had not the same meaning), and put a slice of orange, minus the peel, on each to garnish.

A SHROPSHIRE FRAZE

"Blanch half a pound of Jordan almonds, and beat them fine in a marble mortar, with a little rose water. Beat the yolks of eight eggs, and four of the whites; mix them with a pint of cream, a glass of brandy, and one of white wine, sugar to make it pretty sweet, and as much grated bread as will make it into a thick batter; beat it well up together; have a large frying pan, make it hot with a good piece of butter in it; pour as much of the above as will make it full an inch thick. Let it do very gradually. When done on one side, turn it; grate sugar over it, and send wine sauce in a boat."

The Family Cookery Book, by an Experienced Housekeeper, 1835.

Ground almonds will serve for this, and the quantities are discretionary. I used rather less cream, 6 yolks and 3 whites of egg.

For wine sauce, see the chapter on Sauces.

TO MAKE BURNT CREAM

"Boil a pint of cream with sugar and a little lemon peel shred fine. Then beat the yolks of six and the whites of four eggs separately. When your cream is cooled, put in your eggs, with a spoonfull of orange-flower water and one of fine flour. Set it over the fire keep stiring it till it is thick, put it into a dish; when it is cold sift a quarter of a pound of sugar all over, *hold* a *hot* salamander over it till it is very brown and looks like a glass dish put over your cream.

"This a very good sweet.

"H.F.L-Y Pentrepaul, 1832."

MS Family Cook Book. Loaned by Miss Hull

Another version of this has more specific instructions, and recommends putting the egg yolks only with the flour, cream and other ingredients to boil gently for $\frac{1}{2}$ hour. Remove from heat and add the well-beaten whites. Put the whole into the serving dish, strew well with sugar and place in a moderate oven to rise and glaze.

Although I cannot claim to have tested this personally, I include it for the benefit of cream addicts and those fortunates whose diet may allow such delights. Of course, the flavouring may be varied to taste.

THE BEST WAY OF MAKING FRITTERS

"Take twelve golden pippins, core them and cut them in halves, then steep them in brandy six hours; make a batter from that brandy, adding sugar, beaten cinnamon, rose-water, white wine, and flour. Fry them in lard, and serve them up crisp, with powder sugar over them."

The London Cook, or the Whole Art of Cookery Made Easy and Familiar, by William Gelleroy, Late Cook to her Grace the Dutchess of Argyle. And now to the Right Hon Sir Samuel Fludyer Bart, Lord Mayor of the City of London, 1762.

The apples will take up the brandy better if cored and *sliced*. Try it with Calvados too. Indeed the best way of making fritters! Richard Dolby (qv), writing some sixty years later, gives a similar receipt, but advises paring the apples, cutting off the tops at the stalk end, removing the core and a little flesh, so as to form a cup with a lid. After marinating, these are filled with 'apricot marmalade' (or I suppose any conserve), and then fried in batter.

TO MAKE BOMBARD APPLES

"Take large apples, pare them and scope out the Core, and fill them with preserved apricots and some with Orange Have some Puff paste role'd out very thin and put it round them like Dumplings; bake them in a gentle oven in a dish. Take the whites of eggs very well beat, a spoonfull of orange flower water put to it, double refine'd sugar beat and sifted, and a little starch, and beat it a pretty while and Ice the apples all over with it while they are hot, and set them in a warm place. They make a very pretty side dish; they are not to be used till quite Cold, and the Iceing quite Cold."

The Receipt Book of Mrs Ann Blencowe, Feb ye 26th Anno Dom. 1673.

Ann Blencowe was the daughter of Dr John Wallis, mathematician and cryptographer, and she was 17 years old when she began to compile her own Receipt Book. Two years later she married John Blencowe of Marston, Northants who later became a judge and MP for Brackley. They appear to have kept house in some style, and the book is well larded with references to distinguished and titled friends and their ailments in what she styles The Physical Receipts. Thus *Lady Gage's Receipt for a Dropsy*, which involved a decoction of mustard seed and the green top of Broom. She informs us that

'Mustard seed is a great strengthener of the Bowells and Broom a great Dieretick, so much as to fill a common chamber pot in 24 hours.' *Experto crede.*

In the receipt given above any preserved fruit may be used (those in syrup give the best result), or marmalade, or even whole fruit jam. Fortunately we no longer need to follow Mistress Blencowe's instruction for icing when we have icing sugar readily available. For 6 apples I used 8oz icing sugar, 1 tablespoon of water and a similar amount of lemon juice and proceeded in the ordinary way to coat the apples when they had cooled.

CODLING CREAM

"Take codlings and boil 'em in white wine till y^e are soft, drain all ye liquor from 'em and strain ye pulph thro' a strainer, take 1 pint of cream and boil it and thicken it wth ye yolkes of 2 eggs and while its hot put in ye pulph wch must be season'd wth rose-water and sug^r."

Collection of MS receipts all in same fine hand, circa 1800. *Blanche Leigh Collection, Brotherton Library, University of Leeds, MS* 53.

This is taken from a manuscript cookery and commonplace book in the Brotherton Library (University of Leeds), to which is ascribed the date *circa* 1805. At one end was included a 'Wonderful and most surprising Prophecy' concerning the end of the Napoleonic Wars, which I fear made poor reading, as, in the event, it turned out to be totally inaccurate!

However, the Codling Cream is worthy of more attention. I used Cox's Orange Pippins for their delicious flavour—a pound, peeled and cored, seemed enough—boiled in a sweet white wine (try Spanish 'Sauternes' and not much) and followed the directions for the 'pulph', putting it through a fine sieve. Thicken the pint of single cream with the egg yolks, being careful not to curdle the mixture, then add the apple and a little fine sugar. The rose-water seemed an additional, but unneccessary, refinement. This is best served well-chilled.

TO MAKE HASTY FRITTERS

"Put some Butter into a stewpan and let it heat. Take $\frac{1}{2}$ pint of good Ale and stir into it by degrees a little flour, put in a few currants or chopped apples, beat them up quickly and drop a large spoonful at a time all over the pan. Take care that they do not stick together; turn them with an egg slice; when they are a fine brown lay them on a dish and throw sugar over them."

Manuscript cookery book: Mrs F. Briggs, Wigmore Street, 1825. Blanche Leigh Collection, Brotherton Library, University of Leeds, MS 60.

This is a paraphrase of John Farley's receipt in *The London Art of Cookery* (1783) of which the twelfth edition was published in 1811, and which may well have had a place on Mrs Brigg's kitchen shelf. He adds characteristically: 'You may cut an orange into quarters for garnish.'

TO MAKE FLUMMERY

"One quart of new Milk one ounce of Isinglass, two ounces of blanched Almonds beat in a mortar with Rose water, half the skin of a Lemon, Lump sugar to your taste boil all together very slowly till the Isinglass dissolves, stir

it till near cold then add a glass of white wine, strain it
through a piece of Muslin and put it into Moulds—very
good."

*E. Keyworth's Receipt Book (MS) 1831. Loaned by Miss Yolande
Clements.*

This is the simplest of many versions of what was once a popular
item of diet. It seems to have had its origins in rural cookery, since the
older receipts with this name call for oatmeal soured in warm water
for several days, strained and boiled in milk until curdled! Over the
years it gained sophistication to the point where the oatmeal vanished
and it became a genteel dessert. In the following I have compounded
two or three similar instructions and produced an easily made traditional sweet.

Two pints of milk; 2oz powdered gelatine; a teaspoonful of lemon
juice with a little grated peel; enough granulated sugar to sweeten to
your taste; a glass of sweet white wine or half a glass of brandy. Boil
all together gently, keeping it stirred, for 15 minutes. Add 1oz of
ground almonds if you like the flavour. Take off the heat and strain,
stirring until luke warm. Pour into a basin or suitable jelly mould to
cool and set. One author recommends 'garnish with currant jelly'. I
used cream.

(*Elizabeth Keyworth's Receipt Book*, dated 1831 in flyleaf. Many
recipes are previous to this date; the Keyworths were a Yorkshire
farming family of some substance, for many generations.)

TO MAKE FLUMMERY CAUDLE

"Take a pint of oatmeal, and put it to two quarts of fair
water; let it stand all night, in the morning stir it, and
strain it into a skillet with three or four blades of mace,

and a nutmeg quartered; set it on the fire, and keep it stirring, and let it boil a quarter of an hour; if it is too thick, put in more water, and let it boil longer; then add a pint of rhenish white wine, three spoonfuls of orange-flower water, the juice of two lemons, and one orange, a bit of butter, and as much fine sugar as will sweeten it; let all these have a walm, and thicken it with the yolks of two or three eggs. Drink it hot for breakfast."

The Compleat Housewife or Accomplish'd Gentlewoman's Companion, 15th edition, 1753. By Eliza Smith.

The first part of this receipt is the standard method for making flummery, which much resembled our porridge. When we come to the rhenish wine and other concomitants, the author is giving us a dessert (*breakfast?*) which, in another contemporary version, Mrs Glasse (1747) asserts 'when *cold* it eats very pretty with cyder and sugar'.

Try the alcoholic version well chilled and served with cream.

YELLOW FLUMMERY

"Take two ounces of Isinglass and pour a pint of boiling water over it when cold add a pint of white wine the juice of two lemons and the rind of one, the yolks of eight eggs beat well, put it in a pan and keep stirring it, when it boils strain it through a sieve, and put it into moulds when cold—Mrs Harrison—Good."

E. Keyworth's Receipt Book (MS) 1831. Loaned by Miss Yolande Clements.

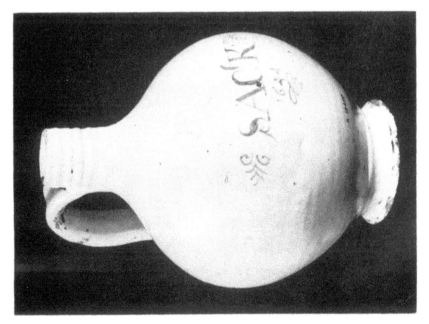

Page 123 (left) *A glazed earthenware 'bombard' of sack, 1654. Cf Henry IV, Part 2 of Falstaff, 'The huge bombard of sack'; (right) seventeenth-century gingerbread mould, showing a lady of fashion*

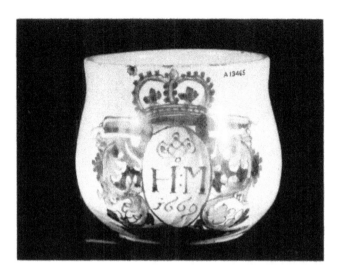

Page 124　(above) *A personalised posset-pot in glazed earthenware;* (below) *sixteenth-century earthenware cooking pot, legged for table service*

I think this would require a little more attention than the bare instructions given. Possibly they were hasty notes jotted down that afternoon when Mrs Harrison came to tea with Elizabeth Keyworth in 1831, and the gossip proved more memorable than the receipt.

For the experimental cook I would suggest the addition of sugar (white wine and lemon juice is surely vinegar), boil up before adding the beaten egg, which should be added at a lower temperature to prevent curdling. In any event it seems unnecessary to strain it, and a similar receipt from another source (called, for some esoteric reason, Dutch Flummery), does not require it.

TO MAKE PAN CAKES

"To a pint of cream put 6 eggs, a Pint of Flour, ½lb of Butter, a little Orange or Rose Water, some Sack Nutmeg and Sugar to your taste and salt; beat it well together, the butter must be melted before you put it in your Cream, put a Bit of Butter in the Pan to fry the first least it should burn but to none of the rest, if you please you may put 8 Eggs but then 4 of the Whites must be left out and you are then to put but 4 Spoonfuls of Flour, put the Butter into a Bit of muslin and when the Pan is hot rub it till it shines."

Dorset Dishes of the 17th Century, collected by J. Stevens Cox, FSA, 1967. Original folio manuscript covering period 1660–80 from the Bragge family of Beaminster and Sadborrow.

Coming as it does from a county long famous for its dairy products, this with its lavish use of cream instead of milk transforms the rather pedestrian pancake into food for the gods. For the somewhat haphazard instructions I can give something more specific.

Beat the 6 eggs thoroughly first, then mix them with a pint of cream; add a tablespoonful of sugar, half a glass of sweet sherry, some grated nutmeg, and a good pinch of salt. Melt 6oz of butter and mix with the cream after it has cooled a little. Then beat the ingredients well with 4oz of flour until the batter is quite smooth. Heat a heavy 6in frying-pan lightly greased with oil or butter and proceed table-spoonful by tablespoonful in the ordinary way, browning both sides. Sprinkle well with sugar and lemon juice and serve hot.

TO MAKE WHIP'D SILABUBS

"Take Wine, Sidor or Ale and put Creame with Sugar Rosemary and Lemon to a little of any of these then squort it to a froath then fill your glasses."

MS Family Cookery Book, circa 1713, *Catherine Richardson. Loaned by Mrs Bowering, Poole.*

Syllabubs, which are again finding place on the modern table, are a good standby for the busy hostess, as they should be made the day before required. The very general directions given two hundred years ago in the above receipt still stand. Here is a more precise method.

To ½ pint of cream add the juice of 2 lemons and 4oz of castor sugar. Whisk thoroughly until it stands up well. Add gradually a glass of sweet white wine (or cider; ale *not* recommended) and beat up again. Fill your glasses and chill overnight or until required.

In this, as in the succeeding recipes, the large and now costly quantities of cream can quite authentically be replaced by milk with a little cream added to enrich it. The whisking, so necessary to this type of sweet, we can now thankfully leave to the various mechanical means at our disposal!

TO MAKE A SILABUB

"Take a quarte of creame sweeten it to your taste squeeze
in a lemmon with a piece of the pill put in halfe a quarter
of a pint of sack a drope of orrindge flour water then take
out your lemmon pill whipe it with a clean whiske as the
froth riseth take it of with a spoon put it in your Glasses
whipe it again it will fill 7 till you have enough."

MS Family Cookery Book, circa 1713. *Loaned by Mrs Bowering,
Poole.*

These directions derive from the same manuscript source (but in
another, later hand) as that on the preceding page. I include it to
show the gradual sophistication of this excellent sweet which originally stemmed from a simple restorative drink, popular in Eliza-
bethan England, which consisted simply in milking the cow directly
into a jug of sweetened ale or wine. As town dairies carried their own
livestock this was not difficult to achieve.

An early mention appears in a small printed book, *The High and
Mightee Commendation of the Vertue of a Pot of Good Ale*, published in
the sixteenth century decrying the innovation of flavouring ale with
hops.

> 'Their ale-berries,* caurdles and possets cach on
> And sullabubs made at the milking pail
> Although they be many, Beer comes not in any
> But all are composed with a pot of good Ale.'

---

* Aleberries, a medicinal drink, are described as 'excellent against the Hecticks'.

SYLLABUBS—MISS ALLEN'S EXCELLENT

"To a pint of white Wine—add a wine Glass full of Brandy—grate the rind of one Lemon the juice of 3 fine or 4 Small Lemons with ten ounces of loaf sugar stir all these ingredients together—& gently pour in a quart of good Cream—let it stand for 2 or 3 hours—put it in a large pan and whisk it well for half an hour—let it remain till the Whey settles put the froth on a Sieve—& whisk up what remains again & again as long as any froth will rise & taking care to place it on the Sieve to drain— Observe, three Pints of Cream with its proportionate ingredients will fill many Glasses—44 glasses."

MS Receipt Book, Catherine Dixon, circa 1811. *Loaned by Miss M. Aldred, FRSA.*

Unless you are giving a very large party, or preparing for a rout at the Assembly Rooms you will not require 44 glasses.

Try it thus:

3 glasses white wine

teaspoonful of cooking brandy

teaspoonful of grated peel

juice of 1 small lemon

1 dessertspoonful of granulated sugar

½ pint carton single cream

Whisk until well blended, and then follow the original receipt. This will suffice for 4 to 6 glasses, and is, as Miss Allen opined, excellent.

AN EXCELLENT SILLABUB

"Fill your Sillabub-pot with Syder (for that is the best for a Sillabub) and good store of Sugar and a little Nutmeg; stir it well together, put in as much thick Cream by two or three spoonfuls at a times, as hard as you can, as though you milk it in, then stir it together exceedingly softly once about, and let it stand two hours at least ere it is eaten, for the standing makes the Curd."

The Compleat Cook. Expertly prescribing the most ready wayes for dressing of Flesh, and Fish, ordering of Sauces or Making of Pastry. London. Printed by E.B. for Nath. Brook at the Angel in Cornhill, 1658.

A cider syllabub! Amateurs may amuse themselves by endeavouring to reproduce the action of milking the cream in as if straight from the udder. Try squeezing it through the nozzle of an icing-bag, or even a basting syringe! Use still, not aerated, cider.

A SILLIBUB CLEAR AT YE BOTOM CREAM IN YE MIDLE AND CURD AT YE TOP

"Take ye white of 4 or 5 eggs and beat em very well with a wisk tied double then put in near ½lb of sifted sug^r beat it in ye eggs till its melted then just put in ye juce of a lemon and beat it together a while, then pour in ½ a pint of sack and beat together, then put in a pint of good thick cream and beat it together a good while, then fill ye glasses wth it and let 'em stand 6 hours at least before you use it."

Collection of MS receipts all in same fine hand, circa 1800. *Blanche Leigh Collection, Brotherton Library, University of Leeds, MS* 53.

SOLID SYLLABUBS

"Take the rind of two or three Lemons & let it steep with half a pound of lump sugar in a pint of sweet wine for a night—add the juice of two or three Lemons strained put this mixture to a quart of Cream carefully stirring it all the time—then beat it with a whisk for half an hour & let it stand to settle before you put it into Glasses—N:B: If the lemons are large two will be sufficient."

MS Receipt Book, Catherine Dixon, circa 1811. *Loaned by Miss M. Aldred, FRSA.*

EVE'S (OR THE RHYME) PUDDING

"To make a good pudding pray mind what you're taught,
Two pennyworth of Eggs when they're 12 for a groat.
6 ounces of Bread—let Poll have ye crust—
The crumb must be grated as small as ye Dust.
Take of ye fruit Mother Eve once did cozen
Well pared and chopt at least half-a-dozen:
6 ounces of Currant from ye grist you must sort
Least you breake out y^r teeth and spoil all ye sport:
6 ounces of Sugar won't make it too sweet,
Some salt and a nutmeg will make it compleat.
3 hours you must boil it without any flutter,
Nor is it quite finished without melted butter."

Manuscript Cookery book by various hands, eighteenth and nineteenth century. Blanche Leigh Collection, Brotherton Library, University of Leeds. MS 31.

6 eggs; 6oz breadcrumbs; 6 smallish chopped apples, cored and peeled; 6oz currants; 6oz sugar, good pinch of salt and grated nutmeg. For 'melted butter' see receipt of that name.

I have included this exactly as it is written, in a childish hand (with the original spelling), from a collection of miscellaneous cookery and medicinal receipts in manuscript, apparently made during the eighteenth and early nineteenth centuries.

I have not, in fact, proved it myself, but for pudding enthusiasts the interest would seem to lie in the use of fine breadcrumbs to bulk it. It might prove a good nursery task, complete with recitation, for young amateur cooks.

H LEONARDS CUSTARD PUDDING

"Put a tablespoonfull of flour into a stewpan with 3oz of butter, mix smoothly over a slow fire adding (by degrees) 3oz of loaf sugar rubbed on lemon and half a pint of new milk, stir untill it thickens but do not let it boil, turn into a basin and when nearly cold add the yolkes of 3 eggs well beaten, line a dish with puff paste with a layer of preserve of any kind on the bottom, apricot is best, pour the custard on the top and bake one hour and quarter in a cool oven —Whisk the whites of 3 eggs with two tablespoonsfull of powder sugar till quite stiff, put on the top and return to the oven for ten minuites just to set and give a pale brown colour.

"Mary Powell's receipt, 1830."

MS Family Cook Book. Loaned by Miss Hull.

The reader will have noted a certain haphazard use of the terms 'pudding' and 'pie', either of which served on occasion for what we would call a tart. Prior to the middle of the last century even this term was generally applied to those rich layered confections the Germans designate as *torte*, or else those small individual pastries as baked by the Queen of Hearts in the nursery rhyme.

AN ORANGE CUSTARD PUDDING

"Take half a pound of candied orange peel, cut it in thin slices, and beat it in a mortar to a pulp; take the yolks of six eggs, and three whites, half a pound of melted butter, and the juice of one orange; mix them together, and sweeten to your taste, bake it with a thin paste under it a little more than half an hour. It is good cold."

The London Cook, or the Whole Art of Cookery Made Easy and Familiar, by William Gelleroy, Late Cook to her Grace the Dutchess of Argyle. And now to the Right Hon Sir Samuel Fludyer Bart, Lord Mayor of the City of London, 1762.

This was a favourite eighteenth-century dessert dish and is given in varying forms by several writers. The following method is a convenient compromise of them all, and is particularly good.

Boil the rind (without pith) of 2 large oranges until soft enough to reduce to a fine paste in the mortar; to this add the juice of 1 orange, 2 tablespoonfuls of sugar and the yolks of 4 eggs and the whites of 3: beat the resultant mixture well (or put in the blender) then pour in gradually 8oz of butter which you have previously melted in a saucepan. Beat up again until the mixture is quite cold and put into custard glasses to set. Decorate with chips of candied orange, and serve chilled.

Optional: Incorporate a dessertspoonful of brandy with the first mix. Substitute boiling cream for the butter (a like quantity) for a richer version or, serve it hot as indicated in the receipt given.

TO MAKE AN ORING FLORINDINE

"Take a quarter of a pound of orring pill lay it in water 2 days then boile it in 2 or 3 waters till it is soft then take it up and dry it in a cloth beat it in a morter till it is like pape then put to it 4 eggs leave out 2 wites halfe a pound of butter as much sugar put in some grated bread a pint of cream with some marrow lay it in a dish with some puff past under and over it the same way make a puding."

MS Family Cookery Book, circa 1713. *Loaned by Mrs Bowering.*

I give this early original (and unpunctuated, kitchen memorandum for its interesting comparison with the 'Orange Custard Pudding' on p 132. Except for the incorporation of the more indigestible cream, marrow and grated bread, it is virtually the same dish as in Gelleroy's printed version nearly a century later.

LADY WHITMORE'S PUDDINGS

"Take $\frac{1}{4}$lb of Butter—turn it to cream, $\frac{1}{4}$lb flour—$\frac{1}{4}$lb powdered white sugar—2 eggs whites & yolks—a little grated Lemon peel—mix well together—put into small tin *high* cups—nearly full—bake in a quick oven serve with wine sauce—N: D——."

MS Receipt Book, Catherine Dixon, circa 1811. *Loaned by Miss M. Aldred, FRSA.*

This bears the stamp of another tea-table discussion—with Lady Whitmore, and the hasty notes made at the time are not very specific. However, it is easy and worth trying, and this is how I would recommend it made.

Take an equal weight of eggs, sifted flour, sugar and creamed butter (ie softened and beaten with the back of a spoon to the consistency of cream). Beat the eggs thoroughly with a whisk in a basin; gradually add the sugar and continue beating; when well mixed blend in the flour gradually, and finally the creamed butter, slightly warmed to amalgamate the better. Put in a little grated lemon peel and mix thoroughly. Pour into well-buttered cups (never mind the height!) and bake for about 20 minutes. The result is not so much a pudding, more like cakes.

A PANCAKE PUDDING

"Take a quart of milk, four eggs, two large spoonfuls of flour, a little salt, and a very little grated ginger and a small glass of brandy; butter your dish and bake it; pour melted butter over it when it comes out of the oven; 'tis a cheap and very acceptable pudding, being less offensive to the stomach than fried pancakes."

The London Cook, or the Whole Art of Cookery Made Easy and Familiar, by William Gelleroy, Late Cook to her Grace the Dutchess of Argyle. And now to the Right Hon Sir Samuel Fludyer Bart, Lord Mayor of the City of London, 1762.

For grated ginger read powdered, and dust with sugar before serving. Beat the mixture well. It will be done as soon as it sets.

A HUNTING PUDDEN

". . . A Pound of Raisins of ye Sun, stoned, a Pound of Sewet, Six eggs, Six Spoonfuls of Flower, a Glass of Brandy, and a little cream. Let it boil 3 or 4 Hours, or as much more as you please.

"N.B. This Receipt is very rich, and it woud be an exceeding nice Pudden with three Times the Quantity of Flower in it."

MS Family Cookery Book. Loaned by Mrs Bowering.

Old cookery books and manuscript notes abound with Hunting Puddings, all slight variations on the same theme. In fact, an elaborated version of our more familiar Plum Duff and doubtless very welcome to the gentlemen in pink after the rigours of the chase, and before the claret. A dish for a cold winter's night made exactly as described.

A BEGGAR'S PUDDING

"Take some stale bread, pour over it some hot water, till it is well soaked; then press out the water, and mash the bread; add some powdered ginger, and nutmeg grated, a little salt, some rose water or sack, some Lisbon sugar, and some currants; mix these well together, and lay it in a pan well buttered on the sides, and when it is well flatted with a spoon, lay some pieces of butter on the top, bake it

in a gentle oven, and serve it hot, with grated sugar over
it. You may turn it out of the pan when it is cold, and it
will eat like a cheese-cake."

*The London Cook, or the Whole Art of Cookery Made Easy and Familiar,
by William Gelleroy, Late Cook to her Grace the Dutchess of Argyle. And
now to the Right Hon Sir Samuel Fludyer Bart, Lord Mayor of the
City of London,* 1762.

This is an interesting variation on our old nursery bread-and-
butter pudding. The addition of sack (sherry), of course, renders it
quite suitable for adults. I found it best chilled, and served with
double-cream. As in so many of these old receipts no quantities are
given, but the practised amateur should have no difficulty in making
his own assessments after the first experiment.

LEMON DUMPLINGS

"$\frac{1}{4}$lb of Suet chopped fine
ditto crumbs of Bread
ditto lump Sugar—2 eggs—one Lemon the rind to be
chopped fine and the juice squeezed tied up close in a
bag & boiled 20 minutes——"

MS Receipt Book, Catherine Dixon, circa 1811. *Loaned by Miss
M. Aldred, FRSA.*

The quantities given will make 4 fair-sized dumplings and can be
adjusted according to the servings required. The addition of a large
tablespoon of flour will lighten them, and, of course, use caster sugar.
Beat up the eggs and add the other ingredients; mix well, finally

adding the lemon juice. If you are using lemon-peel chopped, be certain to shave it so that no pith adheres. More tedious, but better, rasp it on a grater. Divide the mixture into four, tie them in individual floured cloths and boil for 1 hour. Accompany with any sweet sauce. I used the syrup from preserved ginger.

HALF-PAY PUDDING

"Four oz each of flour, suet, currants, raisins, and bread crumbs, two table spoonsful of treacle, and half a pint of milk mix well together, and boil in a mould three hours serve with wine or brandy sauce."

Emma Smith, Alvaston Hall, Derbyshire, November 1855 *MS. Loaned by Mrs Isabel Smith.*

The appealing note of pathos implied in the title is scarcely carried in the end result, which, if you use black treacle, has the taste and appearance of well-made fruit cake. Tie the well-buttered pudding basin in a cloth and boil in a large saucepan.

LEMON SNOW

"$\frac{1}{4}$oz of Isinglass dissolved in a tea cupful of hot water the juice of half (a whole Lemon if not large) the white of 2 eggs, $\frac{1}{4}$ of loaf sugar *sifted*—put altogether into a good size Basin and let it be *whipped, flogged,* or *whisked* for an hour untill it becomes a thick white froth—to be used next day —the peel of the lemon cut very thin and *beat* with it— Amy W——t."

Catherine Dixon 1811 *Canterbury MS Receipt Book. Loaned by Miss M. Aldred, FRSA.*

———————

Those fortunate cooks possessing a mixer who may aspire to make this can account themselves lucky to allow the whipping, flogging and whisking to be done mechanically, while they spend the time shopping or reading a good book. Having dissolved the ¼oz of powdered gelatine with lemon juice as directed, put in the egg whites, grated peel and 4oz of icing sugar, and, I hope, presto! Perhaps they will spare a thought for the luckless servants of the Misses Dixon a hundred and fifty years ago. . . .

TO MAKE CHEESECAKES

"Take eight ounces of sweet Almonds eight ounces of Sugar two ounces of bitter Almonds and the yolks of ten Eggs—the Almonds must be pounded very fine and just wet with water/Rose water is best/to keep them from oiling—beat the Eggs well and mix them together—this quantity will make two dozen—Miss Ann Penkett 1800."

I suppose this mixture is intended to be put into tartlets (*sic*).

Amy Hull Family MS Receipt Book. Loaned by Miss Hull.

———————

I used ground almonds (left out the bitter almonds), reduced the quantities by half and combined it with the yolks of 3 eggs in the emulsifier.

138

ORANGE CHEESECAKES

"Take a large Seville Orange pare it very thin—then boil
the Peel in water twenty minutes change the water
once*—When it is boiled pound it add to it ¼lb Butter
oiled ¼lb Sugar pounded and sifted—add to it the yolks of
six Eggs well beat—when the Butter is warm enough to
run, mix it with the other ingredients and stir them all
together—Line the patty pans with puff paste and then
fill them—Miss A. Penkett."

Amy Hull Family MS Receipt Book. Loaned by Miss Hull.

Another old recipe incorporates the juice as well, adding ½ gill of
cream, a little grated nutmeg and cinnamon.

A FRIARS OMLET

"Boil one dozen apples, as for sauce, stir in a quarter of a
pound of Butter, the same quantity of white sugar when
cold, add 4 Eggs well beaten, put into a baking dish thinly
strewed with crums of bread, so as to stick to the bottom
and sides, then put in the apple mixture, strew crums of
(bread) over the top—when baked turn it out and put
pounded sugar over it—a little grated Lemon peel improves the flavor—For a small Omlet 8 apples and 2
Eggs with a very small piece of Butter is sufficient. From
Anne, Copied by Miss Walford."

* To take out the bitter flavour.

Elizabeth Evans, Walthamstow, MS Receipt Book. Loaned by Mrs Philippa Gregory.

Let us take the quantities for a 'small omlet'. You will need: 4 large apples; 2oz butter; 2 eggs; sugar to taste; grated lemon peel for flavouring.

Peel, core and cut up the apples, and boil in a saucepan in sufficient water to make them just liquid when mashed. Add the sugar, lemon peel, butter and beaten eggs and mix well before transferring to a small fireproof dish, which you have buttered and breadcrumbed. Bake about 55 minutes in a brisk oven or until well set, and dust with sugar before serving.

TO MAKE ORANGE BUTTER

"Take the yolks of ten eggs beat very well, half a pint of Rhenish, six ounces of sugar, and the juice of three sweet oranges; set them over a gentle fire, stirring them one way till it is thick. When you take it off, stir in a piece of butter as big as a large walnut."

The London Cook, or the Whole Art of Cookery Made Easy and Familiar, by William Gelleroy, Late Cook to her Grace the Dutchess of Argyle. And now to the Right Hon Sir Samuel Fludyer Bart, Lord Mayor of the City of London, 1762.

Try this with 4 eggs, being careful not to curdle them, and sugar to taste. This accompanies roast duck very well, served cold

Page 141   *A political caricature by Gillray
showing the popularity—and effect—of punch-
drinking*, 1801

Page 142 *Bringing in the Boar's Head. This
ancient custom noted by Aubrey* (Brief Lives) *in
the seventeenth century was accompanied by a carol.*

> *Apri caput differo*
> *Reddens laudem domino*
> *The boar's head in hand bring I*
> *With garlands gay and rosemary*
> *I pray you all sing merrily*
> *Qui estis in convivio*

TO MAKE A GOOD TANSIE

"Take 15 egges and six wites, beat them well, then put in some sugar, a little sack, beat them again then put in about a pint of creame or a little more, beat them again, then put in it the juice of spinage or of Primrose leaves to make it green with a little juice of Parsley, then put in some more sugar if it be not sweet enough then beat it again a little and so let it stand till you fry it, and when the first course is in, fry it with a little sweet butter, it must be fried enough, then put it into a dish and strow some sugar upon and serve it up."

MS Family Cookery Book, circa 1713. *Loaned by Mrs Bowering, Poole.*

By the eighteenth century many cookery writers omitted the tansy-juice or leaves, with their bitterish, aromatic flavour, but the name persisted without typifying any particular sweet. For this one, use the following adaptation:

4 eggs; ½ pint of cream; 2 dessertspoonfuls sugar; a similar quantity of spinach juice or other vegetable greening (perhaps not primrose leaves); a glass of sherry. Beat up the eggs, then add the cream and sugar. When thoroughly well mixed put in the wine and colouring, give it a final stir and fry in unsalted butter. Sprinkle with more sugar before serving and garnish with slices of lemon.

A PIPPIN TANSY

"Fry as many sliced apples as will cover the bottom of the pan gently in butter. Beat eight eggs with white bread-crumbs, half a pint of cream, add nutmeg and sugar and

I   143

pour over the apples. When 'tis thick, serve up with melted butter and sugar."

Archimagirus Anglo-Gallicus, or Excellent and approved Receipts and Experiments in Cookery. Copied from a choise Manuscript of Sir Theodore Mayerne knight, Physician to the late K. Charles. Magistro Artis; Edere est Esse; *London* 1658.

The quantities seem a little extravagant unless you have a very large saucepan! Cut down to practical measure, this is an interesting variation on the usual apple charlotte.

A TANSIE

"Boyle a q^t of cream or milk wth a stick of cinnamon a quartered nutmeg and a large mace. W^n half cold mix it wth 20 yolks of eggs and 10 whits strain it y^n put to it 4 grated biskits $\frac{1}{2}$lb of butter a p^t of spinnage juice and a little tansie sack and orange flower water sugar a little salt. Gather it to a body over y^e fier and pour it into yor dish being well buttered. W^n tis baked turn it on a pye plate squeese on it an orange grate on sugar garnish it wth slic'd orange and a little tansie made in a plate cut as you please."

Receipts of Pastry and Cookery For the Use of his Scholars, By E. D. Kidder. Who teacheth at his School On Mondays, Tuesdays, and Wednesdays, in the Afternoon, in St Martin's le Grand. And on Thursdays, Fridays, and Saturdays, in the Afternoon, at his School next to Furnival's Inn in Holborn. And Ladies may be taught at their own Houses. London 1702. *Brotherton Library, University of Leeds.*

Master Kidder (whose little book curiously enough contains only three receipts for pastry, despite his title) was possibly demonstrating for his entire class. The quantities should be reduced for a modest table as follows:

½ pint of cream; a pinch of mace and nutmeg; 4 eggs and 2 whites; 2oz butter; a couple of sweet biscuits crushed; a teacupful of spinach juice. You will not be heretic if your garden does not provide tansy. The term became later generally used for dishes of this type. Provide the sack by a little cooking sherry or sweet, white wine. Turn the mixture into a buttered baking dish and stir well over a slow flame until well dissolved. Transfer to the oven and bake for ½ hour on medium heat. The end result should give you a rather creamy pancake.

A WESTMINSTER FOOL

"Cut a penny loaf into thin slices, pour a little sack over them, just enough to wet them, and lay them in the bottom of a dish. Take a quart of cream or milk, six eggs beaten up, a blade of mace, two spoonfuls of rose-water, and some grated nutmeg. Sweeten it to your palate. Put it all together into a saucepan and keep stirring it over a gentle fire. When it begins to grow thick, pour it into the dish. Serve it up cold."

The London Cook, or the Whole Art of Cookery Made Easy and Familiar, by William Gelleroy, Late Cook to her Grace the Dutchess of Argyle. And now to the Right Hon Sir Samuel Fludyer Bart, Lord Mayor of the City of London, 1762.

This turned out to be an interesting hybrid—a custard crossed with a trifle. The original version (above) seemed to lack authority. Try it with Grand Marnier instead of sherry, take care your eggs do not curdle—as the author might say—then chill it well and serve with strawberries.

Quantities: 3 large cupfuls of fresh breadcrumbs; as much liqueur as you can spare; 1 pint milk; 3 eggs; season and sweeten to taste.

Ordinary fruit fools (this word was spelt *fouilles* in Norman-French medieval cookery), eg gooseberry, raspberry, etc are best made by stewing the fruit with sugar or syrup and putting through the blender or foodmill. Chill and stir in cream before serving.

DERBYSHIRE PUDDING

"3oz of flour

3oz of sugar

3 eggs

3oz of butter and half a pint of cream

Put the cream, sugar, butter and a little salt into a stew-pan on the fire, and as soon as this begins to simmer, take it off the fire and add the flour, stir the whole together quickly, and put it on the fire again for five minutes, continuing to stir it. Then the 3 eggs mixed gradually with it, put the whole into a mould, previously spread with butter. Steam it for an hour and a half.

Very good pudding; Margaret Howell's receipt, 1829"

MARLBOROUGH PUDDING

"Crumble at the bottom of a Tin 3 little Sponge Cakes squeeze the juice of a Lemon over them, then put 2oz

Marmalade—dissolve 4oz sifted white sugar in 3oz clarified Butter with the yolks of four Eggs beat all well together. Then pour it over the Marmalade and bake ½ an hour—it must be sent in the moment it comes out of the Oven—Mrs Norton."

Amy Hull Family MS Receipt Book. Miss Hull.

Having beaten the eggs and butter, add the sugar and whisk thoroughly with a little thin cream or milk to obtain the consistency of a light custard. Another author suggests a dash of brandy in this, adding: 'It is an excellent and delicate pudding when properly baked; but like all which are composed in part of custard, it will be spoiled by a fierce degree of heat.' I find the best result with bitter orange marmalade.

POSTATIA-CREAM, VERY GOOD

"Take an ounce of the Kernels of Postatia-Nut, beat them small with two spoonfuls of Orange-flower-Water, and four Yolks of Eggs; boil a quart of Cream, and mix all together: When the Cream is so cool it will not curdle the Eggs, thicken it over the Fire with great Care, and put it into your Glasses."

A Collection of Above Three Hundred Receipts in Cookery, Physick and Surgery; For the Use of all Good Wives, Tender Mothers, and Careful Nurses. By several Hands. London, Printed for Richard Wilkin, at the King's Head in St Paul's Church-yard. MDCCXIV.

In case the reader is puzzled, the anonymous authors were referring to pistachios. If a quart of cream seems extravagant, break it down with milk and lessen the quantity. Mrs Hannah Glasse, writing in 1747, also has this receipt, but crushes her pistachio kernels (½lb!) with a spoonful of brandy in a mortar, and finds a pint of cream enough. She also recommends serving it in a soup-plate, but it looks better in custard glasses, chilled.

UNCLE TOBY'S PUDDING

"New Milk 1 pint, bread crumbs quarter of a pound, butter two ounces; two eggs well beaten, 9 bitter Almonds pounded, 1 Wineglass Sherry; pour the milk boiling hot over the crumbs then add the butter and Almonds with the eggs, wine and sugar to the taste; line a pie dish with paste and bake an hour—Miss White."

E. Keyworth's Receipt Book (MS) 1831. Loaned by Miss Yolande Clements, Reigate

Cakes and Pastry

RECEIPT FOR MAKING MRS NANNCYS PIE CRUST

"Half a pound of Butter, one pound of fine flour, one Egg unbroken—a little pounded sugar the ingredients to be mixed with cold water till the paste is so stiff that it can be only just rolled out, let it stand 2 hours before it is rolled out ready to cover the pie dish. Mrs P."

Elizabeth Evans, Walthamstow MS Receipt Book. Loaned by Mrs Philippa Gregory.

TO MAKE JUMBELS (SHREWSBURY CAKES)

"Take 2 Pound of flour one pound of butter rub the butter in the flour with a pound of sugar put in 2 ounces coreander and cariway seed beat well with 4 eggs 4 spoon-ful of Rose water work it very well together with your hand bake them upon plates; the same way yo do Shrew-berry cakes only leave out the seeds."

MS Family Cookery Book, circa 1713. *Loaned by Mrs Bowering, Poole.*

For the uninitiated, Shrewsbury cakes are made in exactly this way, and the young authoress was evidently confused. What she meant was that her 'jumbels' (for which she had already prescribed the seeds—an essential ingredient of Shrewsbury cakes) were in fact the cakes, and the cakes 'jumbels'. They were cut in rounds with the top of a wine glass and baked on a tin in a slow oven. The high seasoning would make them suitable for 'cakes and ale'.

JUMBELLS

"10oz of flour, rub in 8oz butter and 6oz sugar, mixed with one egg and rolled as you like. A few minutes in a slow oven will bake them—Mrs Marshe."

Manuscript Cookery book by various hands, eighteenth and nineteenth century. Blanche Leigh Collection, Brotherton Library, University of Leeds, MS 51.

Eliza Acton's *Modern Cookery* (1845) gives a more exact recipe for 'Jumbles', viz:

"Rasp on some good sugar and rinds of 2 lemons; reduce it to powder and sift with it as much more as will make up 1lb in weight; mix with it 1lb of flour, 4 well-beaten eggs, and 6oz of warm butter: drop the mixture on buttered tins, and bake the Jumbles in a *very* slow oven from 20 to 30 minutes. They should be pale, but perfectly crisp."

Of the two Mrs Marshe's version would appear the lighter, with less flour and more butter, but apply Miss Acton's cooking directions

VICTORIA CAKES

"½lb flour, ¼lb sugar, ¼lb currants, ¼lb butter, ½ teaspoonful of carbonate of soda.
Mix all, then add 2 large eggs. Bake a quarter of an hour in a slow oven."

MS Family Cook Book, circa 1840. *Loaned by Miss Hull*

If using plain flour in this quick teatime receipt add a ¼ teaspoon of baking powder. Otherwise the same result can be achieved with self-raising flour.

LITTLE SACK PUDDINGS

"Grate two rolls or biscuits in half a pint of cream, thicken this over the fire then take it off, add 4 Eggs some Nutmeg a little Sack or White wine, Salt, Sugar, Currants or not; Bake them in little Pans; when turned out stick them with candid Citron or Almonds."

Manuscript cookery book: Mrs F. Briggs, Wigmore Street, 1825. *Blanche Leigh Collection, Brotherton Library, University of Leeds, MS* 60.

Unable to determine the size of rolls or biscuits indicated, I crushed 6 biscuits of the type called 'digestive' and mixed this with a small carton of double cream, to which I added some milk to make up rather more than ½ pint. Stir this mixture well in a saucepan over moderate heat to thicken (adding more biscuit crumb if necessary).

Off the fire stir in the beaten eggs, half a glass of cooking sherry, a pinch of salt and ground nutmeg, and put in small individual pie tins to bake.

WHINNINGTON CAKES

"½lb of flour; ½lb of loaf sugar; 4oz of butter rubbed into the flour; a few currants or almonds; 3 eggs, leaving out 2 whites; the rind of a lemon and a little mace. Lay them upon tins in lumps. A few minutes will bake them—1836."

Manuscript Cookery book by various hands, eighteenth and nineteenth century. Blanche Leigh Collection, Brotherton Library, University of Leeds, MS 51.

HUNTING GINGERBREAD

"6oz butter, 1lb of Flour, mix them well together. 1oz ginger, some nutmeg, two or three cloves, a little Chyan [cayenne pepper] half a pound of sugar, the like of Treacle and a little candid Lemon."

This and the succeeding two receipts for Parkin are taken from Margaret Walker's Cookery and Commonplace Book, written in Yorkshire between the years 1778 and 1846 and forms part of the Blanche Leigh collection in the library of the University of Leeds. It includes many references to friends and neighbours with whom she evidently exchanged notes. (Thus, Mrs Wardle's receipt for Roche's Embrocation; Mrs Wilson: receipt for Hooping Cough. Also to destroy caterpillars on gooseberries!)

I found the best method of making this excellent old gingerbread was to mix all the dry ingredients first, and then beat in the melted butter, sugar and treacle until the mixture binds sufficiently to press into the cake tin. Bake in a slow oven for about an hour, and turn out when cold.

ELIZABETH SHILLITO'S RECEIPT FOR TREACLE PARKIN, 1804
(*The Shillitos were substantial Yorkshire farmers*)

"3lbs Oatmeal; ¾lb sugar; ½lb Butter; ¼lb lard; 2lb Treacle; 2oz ginger; Lemon, Powdered cinnamon to your taste. 3 Tablespoons of Ale or Brandy. Bake it in loaves. or,
2lb Oatmeal; 2lb Treacle; 1lb raw sugar; 8oz butter; 1oz Ginger. 4 Tablespoons Brandy; 4 of Beer. Rub the butter into the oatmeal; just warm the treacle. The treacle and the butter must be melted together. It is better mixed the night before."

Margaret Walker's Cookery and Commonplace Book, 1778–1846
Blanche Leigh collection in the library of the University of Leeds

These quantities will make a fairly substantial Parkin, but it keeps well and in fact improves by keeping a week before use, if you can resist it! Bake evenly in a slow oven for 1 hour and allow to cool in the tin, which should preferably be large, shallow and square. Use equal parts of black treacle and golden syrup mixed, and knead the whole well into a semi-liquid dough which will just pour into the well-greased tin.

Sauces

A REGALIA OF COWCUMBER

"Take 12 cowcumbers and slice y^m as for eating put y^m in a cource cloth beat and squeese y^m very dry flower and fry y^m brown y^n put to ye clarret gravy savory spice a bitt of butter rouled up in flower toss y^m up thick they are sauce for mutton or lamb."

Edward Dalton MS circa 1750 (148 recipes). From the Brotherton Library MSS collection, University of Leeds. MS 52.

Although I have taken this from a manuscript source, I subsequently encountered it, with the same delightful name, and almost verbatim, in a printed book of a rather later date. It is interesting to speculate who copied whom, but evidently this relishing and unusual sauce was widely used at the time. The quantities would seem to indicate at least a saddle of mutton or a hindquarter of lamb, but for our more modest modern table, one large cucumber will suffice.

Peel and cut the cucumber in fairly thick slices, and extract the water in the ordinary way by salting them well on a plate for 10 minutes and pouring it off. Dry them on a cloth (I don't recommend 'squeesing' them) and fry them in butter or oil. In a saucepan add 2 glasses of red wine to as much stock as you need, and thicken with *beurre manié*. Omit salt from your 'savory spice' but include nutmeg and a suspicion of sugar. A little chopped parsley makes it look pretty; and then your guests, I hope, will not be asking for the mint.

PARSLEY AND BUTTER

"Wash some Parsley very clean, and pick it carefully leaf by leaf; put a tea-spoonful of salt into half a pint of boiling water: boil the Parsley about ten minutes; drain it on a sieve; mince it quite fine, and then bruise it to a pulp.

"The delicacy and excellence of this elegant and inno-cent Relish depends upon the Parsley being minced *very* fine: put it into a sauce-boat, and mix with it, by degrees, about half a pint of good melted butter—only do not put so much flour to it, as the Parsley and Butter over boiled things, but send it up in a Boat.

"*Obs.*—In French Cookery books this is called '*Melted Butter, English Fashion*;' and, with the addition of a slice of lemon cut into dice, a little Allspice and Vinegar, '*Dutch Sauce*'."

Apicius Redevivus or The Cook's Oracle. By William Kitchiner, MD, 1817

MELTED BUTTER

"Keep a pint stew-pan for this purpose only.

"Cut two ounces of butter into little bits, that it may melt more easily, and mix more readily;—put it into the stew-pan with a large tea-spoonful (i.e. about three drachms) of Flour, (some prefer *Arrow Root*, or *Potato Starch*), and two tablespoonsful of Milk.

"When thoroughly mixed,—add six table-spoonsful of water; hold it over the fire, and shake it round every minute (all the while the same way), till it just begins to simmer, then let it stand quietly and boil up. It should be of the thickness of good cream.

"*Obs.*—This is the best way of preparing melted butter; —Milk mixes with the butter much more easily and more intimately than water alone can be made to do. This is of proper thickness to be mixed at table with Flavouring Essences, Anchovy, Mushroom, or Cavice, &c. If made merely to pour over vegetables, add a little more milk to it.

"N.B. If the BUTTER OILS, put a spoonful of cold water to it, and stir it with a spoon,—if it is very much oiled, it must be poured backwards and forwards from the Stew-pan to the Sauce-boat till it is right again.

"MEM.—Melted Butter made to be mixed with flavouring Essences, Catchups, &c. should be of the thickness of light Batter, that it may adhere to the Fish, &c."

Apicius Redevivus or The Cook's Oracle. By William Kitchiner, MD, 1817.

MELTED BUTTER

"Is so simple and easy to prepare, that it is a matter of general surprise, that what is done so often in every English kitchen, is so seldom done right,—Foreigners may well say, that although we have only ONE SAUCE for Vegetables, Fish, Flesh, Fowl, &c.—we hardly ever make that good.

"It is spoiled nine times out of ten, more from Idleness than from Ignorance, and rather because the Cook won't than because she can't do it,—which can only be the case when Housekeepers will not allow Butter to do it with.

"GOOD MELTED BUTTER cannot be made with mere flour and water; *there must be a full and proper proportion of Butter.*—As it must be *always on the Table,* and is THE FOUNDATION OF ALMOST ALL OUR ENGLISH SAUCES; we have

Melted Butter and Oysters,
———————— Parsley,
———————— Anchovies,
———————— Eggs,
———————— Shrimps,
———————— Lobsters,
———————— Capers, &c. &c. &c.

I have tried every way of making it; and I trust, at last, that I have written a receipt, which if the Cook will carefully observe, she will constantly succeed in giving satisfaction.

"*In the quantities of the various Sauces* I have ordered, I have had in view the providing for a Family of half-a-dozen moderate people.

"Never pour Sauce over Meat, or even put it into the dish;—however well made, some of the Company may have an antipathy to it;—Tastes are as different as Faces:—moreover, if it is sent up separate in a boat, it will keep hot longer, and what is left may be put by for another time, or used for another purpose.

"*Lastly.*—Observe, that in ordering the proportions of MEAT, BUTTER, WINE, SPICE, &c. in the following receipts, *the proper quantity is set down,* and that *a less quantity will not do;*—and in some instances those Palates which have been used to the extreme of *Piquance*, will require additional excitement.

"This may be easily accomplished by the aid of that Whip and Spur, which Students of long standing in the School of Good Living are generally so fond of enlivening their palate with, *i.e. Cayenne* and *Garlic*."

Apicius Redevivus or The Cook's Oracle. By William Kitchiner, MD, 1817.

A CAUDLE FOR SWEET PYES

"Take sack and white wine alike in quantity, a little verjuice and sugar, boil it, and brew it with two or three eggs, as butter'd ale; when the pyes are baked, pour it in with a funnel, and shake it together."

The Compleat Housewife or Accomplish'd Gentlewoman's Companion, *15th edition,* 1753. *By Eliza Smith.*

The term 'caudle' was usually applied to a warm gruel made up with oatmeal or groats flavoured with spices, wine etc and given to invalids.

I used an approximation of the above to enhance the flavour of an apple pie thus:

To a gill each of sweet sherry and white wine add the juice of a lemon and a teaspoonful of brown sugar. Dissolve and reduce slightly over heat; take off the fire and thicken with the beaten yolk of 1 egg and pour the mixture into the pie just before serving (but not at oven-heat, or it will curdle).

Page 159   *Sir Kenelm Digby, 'the discursive cavalier'*

Page 160 Wassailing. A Christmas custom in the old days

CELERY SAUCE

"To strong Gravy add Butter and Flour as if you were going to melt it—boil the Celery and cut it in pieces then put in a few oysters or Anchovy a little Catsup and some grated Nutmeg let it boil very well then put in sufficient Cream to make it white and a little white wine let it boil just before you send it to table—Miss A. Penkett."

Amy Hull 1883 *Family MS Receipt Book. Ref: Miss Hull.*

Early recipes involving the use of *melted butter* are referring to a specific sauce-base, similar to a white *roux*. See Dr Kitchiner on the subject, p 155.

GREEN ONION SAUCE

"You must put into your stewpan green onions, pared and cut small, with a little melted bacon, seasoned with a little pepper and salt; moisten it with gravy, and let it stew a moment; thicken your sauce with cullis of veal and ham; let your sauce be of a sharp taste and good relish, and serve it up hot."

The London Cook, or the Whole Art of Cookery Made Easy and Familiar, by William Gelleroy, Late Cook to her Grace the Dutchess of Argyle. And now to the Right Hon Sir Samuel Fludyer Bart, Lord Mayor of the City of London, 1762.

Chop half a dozen spring onions and fry them until soft in bacon fat, with a few small pieces of bacon added. Season well with ground pepper (it will probably be salt enough) and add a little stock. To obtain the sharp taste I added a few drops of Worcester sauce and served as an accompaniment to fried calves' liver.

LIVER SAUCE FOR BOILED FOWL

"Boil hard 2 Eggs, rub the yolks fine with 1 Anchovy or a little Essence, some lemon peel and the liver of the Fowl braided, parsley boil'd and chopt, butter melted, the pulp and juice of a lemon. Make it hot before you put in the lemon."

Manuscript cookery book: Mrs F. Briggs, Wigmore Street, 1825. Blanche Leigh Collection, Brotherton Library, University of Leeds, MS 60.

SAUCE FOR FISH IN LENT, OR AT ANY TIME

"Take a little thyme, horse-radish, a bit of onion, lemon peel, and whole pepper; boil them in a little fair water; then put in two anchovies, and four spoonfuls of white wine; strain them out, and put the liquor into the same pan again, with a pound of fresh butter; when 'tis melted take it off the fire, and stir in the yolks of two eggs well beaten, with three spoonfuls of white wine; set it on the fire again, and keep it stirring till 'tis the thickness of cream, and pour it hot over your fish. Garnish then with lemon and horse-radish."

The Compleat Housewife or Accomplish'd Gentlewoman's Companion,
15th edition, 1753. *By Eliza Smith.*

After a little experiment I evolved from this a very good fish sauce, which in fact bore some resemblance to a *hollandaise* with a more spicy tang.

In a small saucepan put in your herbs, lemon peel, a very little horse-radish or mustard and 5 or 6 peppercorns. Add a 50-50 mixture of dry white wine and water to total $\frac{1}{2}$ pint. Boil until reduced by half, remove and strain. Mix in a basin the yolks of 2 eggs, a large knob of butter (*not* a pound!) and pour over the strained contents of your saucepan. Stir over gentle heat until well mixed, preferably in a *bain-marie*, or a larger saucepan of water. Keep stirring, add a little more white wine and a few small pieces of butter until quite smooth. Serve at once to enliven dull filleted plaice, or as the author says, at any time.

SAUCE FOR STEAKS

"A glass of ale, two anchovies, a little thyme, savory, parsley, nutmeg and lemon peel shred together. When the steaks are ready, pour out the liquor, and put the ale, etc, into the pan with some butter rolled in flour and when hot, strain it over the steaks Have a care the ale is not bitter."

Thomas Grey (The poet), 1761. *Taken from MS letters to the Rev James Brown, Master of Pembroke College, Cambridge, in the British Museum.*

Any bland lager will do for this. Bring it all to the boil with the pan juices, and thicken to taste. Remember 2 anchovies will be 4 fillets, and if they are not to hand use a scant teaspoon of anchovy essence, or even good anchovy paste.

TO MAKE SAUCE FOR A PIGG

"Boile Sage and parsly Shred small in a little water boile in some Corrants then take it of and put in some Gravie with the Brains of the Pigg a little Sugar and vinegar some butter beaten together and put in the Dish."

MS Family Cookery Book, circa 1713. *Ref: Mrs Bowering, Poole B* 001.

From these rather dotty directions (from the manuscript, *June ye* 24, 1713, it would seem they were written by a small girl) I composed an interesting and unusual sauce for roast pork as follows:

Soak in warm, salted water and prepare a set of calf's or sheep's brains in the usual way; stiffen them in simmering water for 5 minutes. Put on one side. In a ½ pint of stock put a handful of chopped parsley and a pinch of sage. Bring to the boil and add 3oz currants or sultanas, a small wineglass of wine vinegar and a tablespoonful of sugar. Let all simmer for a while until the sugar is dissolved and the fruit softened. Meanwhile, mash or liquidise the brains, season with salt and pepper and add to the stock etc. Heat the mixture thoroughly and, before serving, add a little *beurre manié* to thicken.

A pleasing change from perpetual apple sauce?

WINE SAUCE FOR SWEET PUDDINGS

"Boil together gently for ten minutes the very thin rind of half a small lemon, about an ounce and a half of sugar, and a wineglassful of water. Take out the lemon peel and stir into the sauce until it has boiled for one minute an ounce of butter smoothly mixed with a large half-teaspoon of flour: add a wineglass and a half of sherry or Madeira or other good white wine, and when quite hot, serve the sauce without delay."

Modern Cookery for Private Families Reduced to a System of Eays Practice, London 1845. By Eliza Acton

SAUCE FOR BOILED FOWL

"Boil the liver and two eggs hard, shred them very fine, with an anchovy. Grate a little nutmeg and lemon peel, and a very little pepper. Have ready some good melted butter, and boil all up together."

The Family Cookery Book, by An Experienced Housekeeper, 1835.

Boil the eggs hard, but the liver soft (3 minutes) and pound the mixture, with the nutmeg etc, well. Here again see the note on anchovy in 'Sauce for Steaks', p 163, and 'Melted Butter', p 155. Use 2 or 3 livers if possible, to accentuate the flavour.

TO MAKE LEMON-SAUCE FOR BOIL'D FOWLS

"Pare off the rind of a lemon, then cut the lemon into small slices, and take all the kernels out, bruise the liver with two or three spoonfuls of good gravy, then melt some butter, mix it all together, give them a boil, and cut in a little lemon-peel very small. Blanch it with parsley and hard eggs."

The London Cook, or the Whole Art of Cookery Made Easy and Familiar, by William Gelleroy, Late Cook to her Grace the Dutchess of Argyle. And now to the Right Hon Sir Samuel Fludyer Bart, Lord Mayor of the City of London, 1762.

A similar sauce appears in the 19th edition of Hannah Glasse's *Art of Cookery* which included 'new and useful receipts', published 1796.

She suggests (and I concur) blanching the liver and chopping it fine, cooking the liver and lemon etc briefly together and then pouring hot melted butter over it in the sauce-boat. 'Boiling of it' she says 'will make it go to oil'.

A LEAR FOR SAVORY PYES

"Take clarret, gravy, oyster liquor 2 or 3 anchovies a faggot of sweet herbs and an onion boyle it up and thicken it wth brown butter y^{n} pour it into yor pyes w^{n} cald for. . . ."

Edward Dalton MS circa 1750 (148 recipes). From the Brotherton Library MSS collection, University of Leeds. MS 52.

Depending, of course, on the size of your pie, this seemingly simple mixture poured in 'when cald for', ie 10 minutes or so before serving, will transform a chicken pie or even steak and kidney from the workaday to the memorable. For 6 servings use:

Two wine glasses of cooking claret or whatever red wine is in the kitchen bottle; ½ pint of stock; forget the oyster liquor; 4 anchovy fillets well mashed with the back of a spoon, a bouquet garni (tied with thread for retrieving) and a small onion finely chopped up or grated. Bring to the boil and simmer for 15 minutes in a small saucepan. Meanwhile, make a brown *roux* with butter and flour, and to it add gradually your flavoured wine and stock mixture, take out the herbs, and pour into your pie to finish cooking.

VENISON SAUCE

"Boil claret, grated bread, whole cinnamon, ginger, mace, vinegar and sugar up thick."

The London Cook, or the Whole Art of Cookery Made Easy and Familiar, by William Gelleroy, Late Cook to her Grace the Dutchess of Argyle. And now to the Right Hon Sir Samuel Fludyer Bart, Lord Mayor of the City of London, 1762.

At this date claret had superseded sack or sherry as a popular drink, and England was yet to experience the glories of port as we know it. But port, or at the very least Tarragona, is better used in this receipt. Note again the use of breadcrumb as a thickening agent, of which all that remains in modern cookery is 'bread-sauce'.

Half pint of grocer's port; a pinch of ground cinnamon, ginger and mace; dessertspoonful of wine vinegar and brown sugar. Bring to the boil and then stir grated breadcrumb to the consistency desired. This goes well with wild duck.

ANOTHER SAUCE FOR VENISON

"Take claret, water and vinegar, of each a glass, an onion
stuck with cloves, and some anchovies; put in salt, pepper
and cloves, of each one spoonful; boil all these together;
then strain the liquor through a sieve and serve it in the
dish."

*The London Cook, or the Whole Art of Cookery Made Easy and Familiar,
by William Gelleroy, Late Cook to her Grace the Dutchess of Argyle. And
now to the Right Hon Sir Samuel Fludyer Bart, Lord Mayor of the
City of London,* 1762.

See my remark about port in the foregoing. One clove is sufficient
(unless you are an addict, because you already have the flavour with
the onion) and 4 anchovy fillets will eliminate the need for salt. A
pinch of cayenne instead of a 'spoonful' of pepper.

GOOD SAUCE FOR BOIL'D RABBETS, INSTEAD OF ONIONS

"Boil the Livers, and shred them very small, as also two
Eggs not boil'd too hard, a large spoon-full of grated
white Bread; have ready some strong Broth of Beef and
Sweet-herbs; to a little of that add two spoon-fulls of
White-wine, and one of Vinegar; a little Salt, and some
Butter; stir all in, and take care the Butter do not Oil;
shred your Eggs very small."

A Collection of Above Three Hundred Receipts in Cookery, Physick and

Surgery; For the Use of all Good Wives, Tender Mothers, and Careful Nurses. By several Hands. London, Printed for Richard Wilkin, at the King's Head in St Paul's Church-yard. MDCCXIV.

As you are likely to be cooking 1, or at most 2 rabbits, the miniscule livers won't be sufficient, or may even be unusable. I adapted with 6 chicken livers, first turned in butter to stiffen them, then minced, or put through the mixer with the eggs and breadcrumbs. To a cupful of stock (or cheat with a good quality beef stock cube!) add the wine and vinegar, season and stir in a little butter over low heat. This is good with roast chicken too, as an alternative to bread sauce.

CURRANT SAUCE FOR A PIG

"Boil gently about half an hour a little mace, and some black and Jamaica pepper corns, and a small onion, in half a pint of water; strain it; then lay in some slices of crumbs of bread; let it boil to a pulp with two ounces of currants, nicely washed and picked; beat them together; add a glass of white wine and a little nutmeg, with a good piece of butter; boil it up, and send it in a tureen."

The Family Cookery Book, by An Experienced Housekeeper, 1835.

I think by Jamaica pepper is meant, allspice. Sultanas give a better flavour and I used a sweet wine (Spanish 'sauternes'). The end result is a type of bread sauce and quite successful with roast pork, or chops.

MUSTARD

"My Lady Holmeby makes her quick fine Mustard thus: Choose true Mustard seed: Dry it in an oven, after the Bread is out. Beat and searce it to a most subtle powder. Mingle Sherry-sack with it, (stirring it a long time very well, so much as to have it of a fit consistence for Mustard) then put a good quantity of fine Sugar to it, as five or six spoonfuls, or more, to a pint of Mustard. Stir and incorporate all well together. This will keep a long time. Some do like to put to it a little (but a little) of very sharp Wine-vinegar."

The Closet of the Eminently Learned Sir Kenelm Digby, Kt, Opened
London, 1669.

If you have a mortar and pestle, this is an interesting and worthwhile exercise. It has a fine authority with ham, hot or cold, brawn or pickled pork. I used 3 teaspoons of fine Demerara to make a ½ pint. Any medium cooking sherry will serve. But don't be tempted to use Colman's mustard. Mustard seed, with the husks, well pounded, gives a different end result. (Of Lady Holmeby I can find no trace, but to have one's memory perpetuated in mustard is surely more abiding than marble.)

Drinks

"Some men's whole delight is to take tobacco and drink
all day long in a tavern or ale house, to discourse, sing,
jest, roar, talk of cock and bull over a pot.

"To obtain sleep: 'I say a nutmeg and ale, or a good
draught of muscadine with a toast and nutmeg, or a posset
of the same which many use in a morning, but methinks
for such as have dry brains, are much more proper at
night.' "

Robert Burton's *Anatomy of Melancholy*, 1652

To attempt a survey of popular drinks in England covering three
centuries, even those which might be adapted to present-day use,
would compass an entire and specialised work. The importance attached to drinking by all Englishmen can hardly be over-emphasised,
and our forebears would appear to have used their undoubted talents in
this direction to a prodigious extent. There was almost nothing from
which they would not endeavour to extract a palatable tipple, and
their experiments appear to have led them up some very strange paths
indeed. It is as well to remember that spirits, as we know them, were
little used before the eighteenth century, when the still-room was
principally devoted to domestic medicines and perfumes. Although
vast quantities of native beer, ale and imported wines were consumed

au naturel, the popular palate was often tempted to stray from these pedestrian paths, and the most fearsome mixtures compounded. Merely to read these ancient formulas is a dizzying experience. Here is one to illustrate the point:

> "Cock Ale: Take a cock of half a year old, kill him and truss him well, and put into a cask 12 gallons of Ale to which add 4lbs Raisins of the sun well picked, stoned, washed and dried; sliced Dates ½lb; nutmeggs and mace 2oz. Infuse the Dates and Spices in a quart of Canary 24 hours, then boil the cock in a manner to a jelly, till a gallon of water is reduced to two quarts: then press the body of him extremely well, and put the liquor into the cask where the Ale is, with the spices and fruit, adding a few blades of Mace: then put to it a pint of new Ale yeast, and let it work well for a day, and, in two days you may broach it for use, or, in hot weather the second day; and if it proves too strong, you may add more plain Ale to palliate this restorative drink which contributes much to the invigorating of Nature."

Other favourite drinks in the seventeenth century rejoiced in such mouth-watering titles as Clamber-clown, Hugmatee, Stickback, Knock-me-down, Foxcomb, Stiffle, Blind Pinneaux, Stephony and Bragot, which were principally ale with assorted additives such as honey, spices, herbs and fruit. One is obliged to conclude that the brewer's product was not always what it might have been, and being frequently brewed without hops may have been a trifle insipid. Such strange amalgams apart, however, there were a number of drinks, now forgotten save perhaps in some remote country houses, which are worthy of closer examination and experiment by the dedicated modern tippler and party-giver. In the following pages are given a number of these, to several of which I can add *probatum est.*

When comparing life today with the earlier periods under review, the most outstanding difference is, simply, water. For a century now water has been fit to drink from piped supplies—if only as an additive. Before that nobody but the destitute would drink water and hazard his life. Ale for breakfast, wine at other meals was what Queen Elizabeth drank, and her subjects likewise. The astonishing fact is that there was almost the same quantity of wine imported for a sparsley populated and largely rural country as for the sixty millions of modern industrial England.

While domestic drinking was widespread among the wealthier classes, the general popularity of tavern drinking can be, in some measure, ascribed to the extreme discomfort of the living quarters of the average citizen and countryman, with their small rooms, low ceilings, no windows as we know them, no plumbing, rush lights and perpetually smoking open fires. It was, in fact, a similar circumstance which gave rise later to the Victorian 'gin palace'. The popularity of sack, which will be noticed in a great number of these old receipts, began to wane toward the end of the seventeenth century, to be replaced by claret. To quote Antony à Wood, the querulous and eccentric Oxford antiquarian, in his diary for October 1686: 'Canary wine now sold in London for 1s. 6d. per quart, because all drink claret . . . so that wheras before the warr nothing but sack and mallagoes [malaga] were drunk and claret not at all (only burnt for funerals) now claret generally and sack seldome.' The estimable Samuel Pepys, indulging in a little self-congratulation, would seem to endorse this, as, writing a few years earlier on the subject of his cellar, he notes: 'At this time I have two tierces of claret [a tierce contained one third of a pipe of 105 gallons] two quarter casks of canary . . . another of malaga, and another of white wine, all in my wine cellar together, which I believe none of my friends of my name now alive ever had of his own at the one time.' But if sack left the table, it went no further than the kitchen, as its use is called for constantly in the cookery books of a hundred years later. But except for a staple ingredient of many possets, which can hardly be classified as drinks, there is little mention by the old writers of its use in the cups, mixtures and punches of which they were so fond. It is to these latter that I hope to draw the attention of the more adventurous drinker.

I forbear to weary the reader with the countless old receipts for home-made wines, more especially since the present-day revival of this activity makes it unnecessary. But, as today, the high price of imported wines stimulated intense domestic activity in this direction. John Farley (qv) lists directions for over forty, including such dubious titles as Vino Pontificalo and English Champagne among the fruit and vegetable varieties. However, even contemporary opinion was sometimes adverse. An irate husband wrote to Addison and Steele's *Spectator* in the early eighteenth century about his wife's 'detestable catalogue of counterfeit wines', saying they were not even economical 'as they seldom survive a year and are thrown away!'

A Commendation of the Virtues of Sack

"A good sherris-sack hath a two-fold operation in it. It ascends me into the brain: dries me there all the foolish and dull and crudy vapours which environ it; makes it apprehensive, quick forgetive, full of nimble fiery and delectable shapes, which, deliver'd o'er to the voice, the tongue, which is the birth, becomes excellent wit. The second property of your excellent Sherris is, the warming of the blood; which, before cold and settled, left the liver white and pale, which is the badge of pusillanimity and cowardice: but the sherris warms it and makes it course from the inwards to the parts extreme. It illumineth the face, which, as a beacon, gives warning to all the rest of this little kingdom, man, to arm; and then the vital commoners and inland petty spirits muster me all to their captain, the heart, who, great and puffed up with this retinue, doth any deed of courage; and this valour comes of sherris. So that skill in the weapon is nothing without sack, for that sets it awork; and learning, a mere hoard of gold kept by a devil till sack commences it and sets it in act and use."

William Shakespeare, 1597. *From Henry IV, Part 2, iv, iii.*

It is, perhaps, interesting to note that in 1972 Spanish exports of sherry reached an all-time record.

TO MAKE A SACK POSSIT

"Take 12 eggs 6 whites beat them straine them put to them halfe a pint of sack halfe a pound of sugar put it in a Basin set it on a charcole fire keep it stiring one way till it is ready to boile then set it by take a quart of creame boile it with a little cinnamon and nutmegg then pour it into your sack boiling as high as you can hold it give it stir about cover it on the fire a halfe a quarter of an hour."

MS Family Cookery Book, circa 1713. *Loaned by Mrs Bowering, Poole.*

The Posset, which Dr Johnson described as 'milk curdled with wine and other acids' is found in countless versions in all old cookery books. A prime example of *tot homines tot sententiae.*

I have given the above example, as it appears an elaboration of a much earlier version often quoted as 'Sir Walter Raleigh's Posset' made thus:

Bring to the boil ½ pint of sherry and add gradually a quart of boiling milk. Stir the mixture well and flavour with grated nutmeg. Put in a heated bowl, cover, and stand by the fire for 2 or 3 hours.

The eggs given in the original receipt seem to be a later refinement and I have made this almost as given but using only 6 whole beaten eggs and milk rather than cream. Something for the end of a party on a cold winter's night.

TO MAKE A POSSET WITH ALE
King William's Posset

"Take a quart of cream, and mix it with a pint of ale, then beat the yolks of ten eggs, and the whites of four; when they are well beaten, put them to the cream and ale; sweeten it to your taste, and slice some nutmeg in it; set it over the fire, and keep it stirring all the while; when it is thick, and before it boils, take it off, and pour it into the bason you serve it in to the table."

The Compleat Housewife or Accomplish'd Gentlewoman's Companion, 15th edition, 1753. By Eliza Smith.

If you are not entirely deterred by the regal extravagance quoted, you can make a good ale posset quite cheaply.

Heat up a pint of milk until just before boiling and stir in the yolks of 2 eggs and a small knob of butter with castor sugar to taste. Heat a pint of good bitter (preferably not the variety termed 'Keg') and pour into the mixture. Stir and heat to the point where it thickens. Dust with nutmeg and serve.

TO MAKE THE POPE'S POSSET

"Blanch and beat three quarters of a pound of almonds so
fine, that they will spread between your fingers like butter,
put in water as you beat them, to keep them from oiling;
then take a pint of sack or sherry, and sweeten it very well
with double refined sugar; make it boiling hot, and at the
same time put half a pint of water to your almonds, and
make them boil, then take both off the fire, and mix
them very well together with a spoon; serve it in a *china*
dish."

The Compleat Housewife or Accomplish'd Gentlewoman's Companion,
15th edition, 1753. *By Eliza Smith.*

This is not really a posset in the accepted sense, but rather a hot
restorative. If you are tempted to try it, use ground almonds and sweet
(cheap) sherry in the proportionate quantities to suit your experiment.
As you will have boiled off most of the alcohol it might be given to
sophisticated children as a birthday treat without regard to religious
denomination.

HOW TO MAKE METHEGLIN

"Take what quantity of water you please and to every
gallon of water a quart of honey then put it on ye fire and
put into it nutmegs cloves mase and double the quantity of
these in ginger as the scum riseth take it of: lett it boyl till
ye scum has left Rising then take it of: and 12 hours after
put in a small quantity of yeast and 24 hours after tun it up
and in a fortnights end bottle it."

MS Family Cookery Book, circa 1713. *Loaned by Mrs Bowering,*
Poole.

The quantity and variety of aromatic herbs is arbitrary, depending on the maker's taste, but ginger should predominate and thus make it a different drink from mead. The amateur wine-maker will know that the addition of egg whites will raise the scum.

For the curious, it may be of interest to note that Samuel Pepys records on 25 July 1666 (after dining 'at the back stayres' of White-hall Palace on the remains of the King's dinner 'mighty nobly'), '. . . with most brave drink, cooled in Ice (which at this hot time was welcome); and I, drinking no wine, had Metheglin for the King's own drinking, which did please me mightily.'

DELICIOUS MILK LEMONADE

"Dissolve six ounces of sugar in a pint of boiling water, and mix with them a quarter of a pint of lemon-juice, and the same quantity of sherry; then add three-quarters of a pint of cold milk, stir the whole well together, and pass it through a jelly-bag till clear."

Modern Cookery for Private Families. Reduced to a System of Easy Practice. By Eliza Acton, 1845.

Doubtless this refreshing and mildly stimulating version would be served on a summer's afternoon on the croquet lawn. Substitute a bottle of sherry, chill well, and you have a good cold punch.

CURRANT SHRUB

"A pint and a half of Currant juice 1¼lbs loaf sugar, one bottle Rum put it into a jar with a few bitter Almonds,

and let it stand 3 days stirring 4 times a day—run it thro'
blotting paper, and bottle it—D. Nicomarch."

E. Keyworth's Receipt Book (MS) 1831. *Loaned by Miss Yolande
Clements, Reigate.*

———————————

Shrub at one time had a place on every bottle shelf, and I have often
seen smoke-darkened bottles bearing this label in remote country
pubs. It was normally based on orange juice and peel, fortified
with rum, and this version was evidently made with black currant
juice. It is indeed a natural combination, for what tavern-frequenter
has not heard of, if not tasted, rum and orange, and rum and black
currant?
    If you are thus extending your bottle of rum, use demerara sugar.

THE JUSTICE'S ORANGE SYRUP FOR
PUNCH OR PUDDINGS

"Squeeze the Oranges, and strain the juice from the pulp
into a large pot; boil it up with a pound and a half of fine
Sugar to each pint of juice, skim it well, let it stand till
cold, and then bottle it, and cork it well.
    "*Obs.*—This makes a fine, soft, mellow-flavoured
Punch; and, added to melted butter, is a good relish to
Puddings."

Apicius Redevivus or The Cook's Oracle. By William Kitchiner, MD,
1817.

CAMBRIDGE MILK PUNCH

"Throw into two quarts of new milk the very thinly-
pared rind of a fine lemon and half a pound of sugar; bring
it slowly to boil, take out the rind, draw it from the fire,
and stir quickly in a couple of well-whisked eggs which
have been mixed with less than half a pint of cold milk
and strained through a sieve; the milk of course must not
be allowed to boil after these are mixed with it. Add
gradually a pint of rum, and half a pint of brandy, mill the
punch to a froth, and serve it immediately with quite
warm glasses."

*Modern Cookery for Private Families Reduced to a System of Easy
Practice. By Eliza Acton,* 1845.

———————————

There are many versions of this seductive drink, some incredibly
complicated and involving a week's attention until finally bottled, and
thereafter a long period to mature. The above drinks well and the
author notes 'the sugar and spirit can be otherwise apportioned to the
taste'.

The solitary drinker can content himself with putting a teaspoon
of sugar into a tumbler, adding half a wine glass each of rum and
brandy and topping up with boiling milk.

UNCLE TOBY PUNCH

"Rub the rind of one lemon on two lumps of sugar in a
large tumbler with the juice of the lemon. Dissolve this in
one wine-glass of hot water, then add one glass of brandy,
one glass rum, two glasses of hot stout. Mix well, strain
and add more sugar if necessary."

The Flowing Bowl, by Edmund Spenser, published in the nineties of the last century and based on old receipts.

Who was the redoubtable Uncle Toby? His name crops up from time to time in the matter of our forefathers' food and drink, but no clue to his identity. Was it he who possibly modelled for the first jug of that name? We shall never know. But there, I fancy, is his image immortalised.

TO MAKE ALE DRINK QUICK
(*ie bright and lively, Ed*)

"Take six wheat corns and bruise them and put into a bottle of Ale: it will make it exceeding quick and stronger."

The Closet of the Eminently Learned Sir Kenelm Digby, Kt, Opened. 1669.

I include this as being of some interest to the growing body of enthusiasts and devotees of 'home-brewed' to which, of course, it was originally applied.

LAMBS-WOOL

"To make this beverage, mix the pulp of half a dozen roasted apples with some raw sugar a grated nutmeg and a small quantity of ginger; add one quart of strong ale made moderately warm Stir the whole together, and if sweet enough is fit for use. The mixture is sometimes served up in a bowl, with sweet cakes floating in it."

The Curiosities of Ale and Beer, by John Bickerdyke, published about 1860.

To illustrate the antiquity of this receipt the author quotes the following lines:

> 'A cupp of lambswool they drank unto him then,
> And to their bedds they past presentlie.'

from Thomas Percy's *Reliques of Ancient Poetry*, 1765.

RUM BOOZE

"4 Egg-yolks well beaten with powdered sugar in a basin. Take half a bottle of sherry. Add thereto the grated peel of $\frac{1}{2}$ a lemon, $\frac{1}{2}$ a nutmeg grated, a stick of cinnamon and sugar to taste. Put the whole in a saucepan on the fire bring to the boil and remove to a vessel with a spout to it and add one glass of rum. Pour this gradually on to the eggs, add more sugar if required and beat to a white froth before serving."

Christ's College, Cambridge. Traditional.

THE WASSAIL BOWL

"Into the bowl is first placed $\frac{1}{2}$lb of sugar in which is placed one pint of warm beer; a little nutmeg and ginger are then grated over the mixture, and four glasses of sherry and five pints of beer added to it. It is then stirred, sweetened to taste and allowed to stand covered for two to three hours.

Roasted apples are then floated on the creaming mixture and the wassail bowl is ready."

The Curiosities of Ale and Beer, by John Bickerdyke, published about 1860.

The author adds: 'This receipt—the best of some half-dozen before us—is the one adopted at Jesus College, Oxford, where, on the festival of St David, an immense silver-gilt bowl, presented to the college by Sir Watkin W. Wynne in 1732, is filled with this admirable composition, and passed round the festive board.'

TEWAHDIDDLE

"A pint of Table Beer (or Ale, if you intend it for a supplement to your 'Night-Cap', a tablespoonful of Brandy, and a teaspoonful of Brown Sugar, or Clarified Syrup—a little grated Nutmeg, or Ginger may be added, and a roll of very thin-cut Lemon-Peel.

"*Obs.*—Before our readers make any remarks on this Composition, we beg of them to taste it: if the materials are good, and their palates vibrate in unison with our own, they will find it one of the pleasantest beverages they ever put to their lips,—and, as *Lord Ruthven* says, 'this is a Right Gossip's Cup that far exceeds all the Ale that ever MOTHER BUNCH made in her Life-time'—see his Lordship's *Experiments in Cookery* etc. London 1654."

Apicius Redivivus, or The Cook's Oracle, 1817. *By Dr William Kitchiner*

This was given (in larger proportions) at a party. After experimentation, I found it best chilled. Being the forbidden mixture of grape and malt, it is indeed a 'gossip's cup'.

Cheese and Bread

TO POT CHESHIRE CHEESE

"Put three pounds of Cheshire cheese, into a mortar, with half a pound of the best fresh butter you can get, pound them together, and in the beating add a gill of rich Canary wine and half an ounce of mace finely beat, then sifted fine like a fine powder. When all is extremely well mixed, press it hard down in a gallipot, cover it with clarified butter, and keep it cool. A slice of this exceeds all the cream-cheese that can be made."

The London Cook, or the Whole Art of Cookery Made Easy and Familiar, by William Gelleroy, Late Cook to her Grace the Dutchess of Argyle. And now to the Right Hon Sir Samuel Fludyer Bart, Lord Mayor of the City of London, 1762.

If you consider this to be a waste of good Madeira, try it with cooking Marsala, which is fortified with brandy anyway. Adjust the quantities to your needs, and call it, as I did, the Duchess's Cheese, after her Grace of Argyll.

AN ENGLISH RABBIT

"Toast the bread brown on both sides, and lay it in a plate before the fire, then pour a glass of red wine over it, and let it soak the wine up; then cut some cheese very thin, lay it pretty thick over the bread, and put it in a tin oven before the fire, and it will be presently toasted and browned."*

* Serve these rabbits up hot.

The Practice of Cookery, Pastry, Confectionary, Pickling, Preserving etc, 1795. *By Mrs Frazer. Ref: Rosemary Waterhouse W* 001.

I can recommend this as an alternative supper-dish to the Welsh variety. Try it with (grocer's) port, Double Gloucester cheese and under the grill.

Incidentally, Mrs Frazer lifted this almost verbatim from Hannah Glasse (1747). One of the latter's editors, in a later edition (1796), complains bitterly: '. . . if all they [other writers] have borrowed from our book and put into theirs were to be taken away, many a large and high-priced publication would shrink to a size no greater than a child's spelling-book.'

RAMEQUINS (CHEESE)

"Take a quarter of a pound of Cheshire cheese (grated), the same quantity of Gloucester cheese, and beat them in a mortar, with a quarter of a pound of fresh butter, the yolks of four eggs, and the inside of a French roll, boiled in cream till soft; when all is beaten to a paste, mix it with the whites of the eggs, previously beaten, and put the paste into small paper cases, made rather long than square, and put them to bake till of a fine brown. They should be served quite hot. You may, if you think proper, add a glass of white wine."

The Cook's Dictionary, and Housekeeper's Directory: A New Family Manual of Cookery and Confectionery, on A Plan of Ready Reference Never Hitherto attempted. By Richard Dolby, Late Cook at The Thatched House Tavern, St James's Street. 1st edition 1830.

In testing this, I did 'think proper' and added ½ glass of dry white wine. For some less discerning palates a few drops of Worcester Sauce may improve it. This looks and cooks much better in those glazed earthenware ramekins generally obtainable today, and an essential of any modern *batterie de cuisine*.

BUTTER MILK BREAD

"2lbs of flour
80 grains of Carbone of soda dissolved in ½ teacup of warm water, put it into a pint of sour buttermilk, stir it *instantly* and put it into the flour. Make it up *directly* and put it into the oven.

"The whole process of making this loaf requires 3 minutes—the loaf will weigh 3lbs when baked."

MS Family Cook Book, circa 1804. Loaned by Miss Hull.

Allow the buttermilk (which we can now purchase in cartons at the supermarket) to sour in a warm place.

In a pint of this dissolve ½ teaspoon of carbonate of soda and a pinch of salt. This is best done by pouring from one basin to another several times before adding to the flour. Work it quickly into a light dough, divide it into two loaves and bake straight away in a preheated high oven for an hour. This is a change from the better-known soda bread, and is identical with that made by some charcoal burners employed by me in Kent some years ago, and the buttermilk begged from our dairy. It keeps well.

Dinner at Mr Pepys's

DINNER WITH SAMUEL PEPYS AND HIS WIFE

It may amuse some readers to entertain their friends to a Pepysian dinner, a conceit which I confess to having used more than once. In attempting an approximation of the Pepys's fare in the following pages, one may reasonably skip the six roasted chickens, unless you serve a *poussin* apiece to follow the tripe or fish. A less tiresome substitute would be 'a pullet hashed' which Mr Pepys consumed at dinner (among other things) on 3 November 1661. This, in the old cookery-books so closely resembles our modern chicken *à la crème* as to make no odds.

The shoulder of venison may prove a little too much for modate appetites, unless it is for a largy party. It is best boned and rolled, and basted with port and gravy, and will take some hours to cook. As for 'the umbles baked in a pie', you will have to number a laird among your acquaintances to obtain the kidneys, liver and skirts. In the old days umble pie was in any case considered somewhat second-rate, as instance the derogatory expression still used today of making a proud opponent 'eat humble pie'. By the same token it is amusing to note that Pepys offered this to Sir William Penn, Commissioner of the Navy, and a neighbour and colleague of Pepys for whom he harboured an intense dislike. (It was his son who was to become the famous Quaker leader who emigrated and gave his name to Pennsylvania.)

The diarist makes frequent mention of meals he enjoyed—and otherwise—both at home and in the various taverns where he frequently conducted his business or was 'mighty merry' with friends. There are many references to chines of beef, mince pies, lobsters, oysters, strawberries and cream, in fact most of the things we still eat today. In the menus given I have selected a few items which now rarely appear on the English table, but which I, at least, have found enjoyable.

THE PEPYS'S DINNER, 24 *OCTOBER*, 1662

The most excellent dish of tripes as done at my Lord Crew's.
" . . . so home and dined with my wife upon a most excellent dish of tripes of my own directing, covered with mustard, as I have heretofore seen them done at my Lord Crew's."

The 1st Baron Crew was the father-in-law of Pepys's patron, the 1st Earl of Sandwich, invariably referred to as 'my Lord'

"Take about two pounds of cleaned tripe and cut it in pieces some two inches square. Boil three large Spanish onions, halved, in water until tender; then put in your tripe and cook a further fifteen minutes, boiling. Pour off almost all the liquor, thicken the remainder with flour and butter, and mix in a good desertspoon of mild mustard, and serve as hot as possible, garnished with lemon slivers."

(Based on a receipt of Mrs Hannah Glasse, 1747.)

THE PEPYS'S DINNER FOR FIVE GUESTS, 26 MARCH 1662, ON THE OCCASION OF HIS WEDDING ANNIVERSARY

". . . I had a pretty dinner for them, viz: a brace of stewed carps, six roasted chickens and a jowle of salmon, hot, for the first course—a Tanzy and two neat's tongues and cheese for the second."

A BRACE OF STEWED CARPS

"Scrape them clean, gut them and put the roes in a pint of good stale beer (malt vinegar will do. Ed.) to preserve all the blood, and boil the carp gently in a fish-kettle of salted water. In the meantime, into a large saucepan strain the vinegar and add to it a pint of red wine, a little mace, some whole peppercorns, a small onion stuck with cloves, a sliver of lemon-peel and a *bouquet garni*, together with a crushed anchovy and a pinch of horse-radish (the dried variety will equate, Ed.) Simmer this for fifteen minutes or so with the lid on. Strain again and add to it half the hard roe well beaten, two tablespoons of mushroom ketchup, and four ounces of butter. Let the whole boil up and stir it until the sauce thickens and the roe is cooked. Test for salt. With the remainder of the roe beat up an egg adding a pinch of nutmeg and a squeeze of lemon. Form into little cakes and fry in butter. When the carp is cooked pour the sauce over it on the serving dish and send to the table with fried *croûtons* and lemon slices, surrounded by the roe-cakes."

191

(Based on a receipt of Mrs. Hannah Glasse, 1747, styled: 'To Stew a Brace of Carp'.)

The redoubtable Mrs Glasse will again supply us with a receipt *To dress a Jowl of Pickled Salmon,* which was probably what Pepys's guests enjoyed. The jowl is the head and a thick piece of shoulder of any large fish. After soaking overnight to extract the salt, she advises cooking it in a standard fish *court-bouillon* of wine, vinegar, onion and herbs, to which she adds 4oz of butter rolled in flour and then keeping the salmon hot, reduces the cooking liquor by half; strain and pour over as a sauce. Fried parsley to garnish. Obviously, as you are using fresh salmon, you will proceed without the preliminary soaking, and for the uninitiated, I would suggest a *court-bouillon* composed as follows: 1 pint of water; 1 pint dry white wine or dry cider; 1 tablespoon wine vinegar; a few slices of onion and a carrot chopped; 2 teaspoonfuls of *gros-sel* or sea-salt; a few peppercorns and a bayleaf; a pinch of thyme and a little parsley. Simmer slowly for ½ hour before thickening. (Adjust the amount of liquid to just cover the fish.)

As your guests are unlikely to relish two fish dishes simultaneously, you will obviously serve one or the other. For the sweet try the 'Pippin Tansy' on p 143.

THE PEPYS'S DINNER ON 5 JULY, 1662

"At noon had Sir W. Penn (who I hate with all my heart for his base and treacherous tricks, but yet I think it not policy to declare it yet) and his son Wm. to my house to dinner, I having some venison given me a day or two ago, and so I had a shoulder roasted, another baked, and the umbles baked in a pie."

I have referred to this dinner in my preliminary remarks (p 189). For six people the amount seems excessive, but, as so often in those days, the quantity of food presented was often in accordance with the host's place in society, the remains were given to the deserving poor, or finished by the servants.

Some Biographical Notes

ROBERT MAY, 1588-?

Son of a professional cook, and the first cook to be mentioned in any book, he remained a cook all his life. Although his education was limited, it is said 'he was a better gentleman than many'.

Born at Wynge (Wenge) Buckinghamshire, the country seat of Sir William Dormer where his father was the head cook, and at ten years old he was sent to Paris by his patroness, 'Old' Lady Dormer as she was known. There he spent five years, possibly indicating that even then French cuisine was of some importance to the professional cook.

In 1603 he returned to start his apprenticeship, and was articled for seven years to Arthur Hollingsworth of Newgate Market, cook to the Grocer's Company and The Star Chamber. He returned to Wynge to serve under his father until Lady Dormer died.

He then entered service in many great houses among which were those of Lord Castlehaven, Lord Lumley, Lord Mountague in Sussex, Countess of Kent, Lord Rives, John Ashburnam (who was Charles I's confidential agent), Sir Charles Lucas, and finally: 'The Rt Hon the Lady Englefield where he now liveth.' This was at Sholeby, Leicestershire where, aged 71, he wrote in 1660 *The Accomplisht Cook, approved by Fifty Years Experience and Industry of Robert May in his Attendance on Several Persons of Honour*. The book made an instant success and ran to eleven editions (the last in 1685). In the original, as frontispiece, is his portrait with the following lines beneath:

What! wouldst thou view in but one face
all hospitalitie, the race
of those that for the Gusto stand,
whose tables as whole Ark command
of Nature's plentie, wouldst thou see
this sight, peruse May's booke, tis hee.

SIR THEODORE TURQUET DE MAYERNE MD, 1573–1655

Sir Theodore Turquet de Mayerne was born in Geneva in 1573 and his father was a French Protestant historian from Piedmont. He studied at the University of Heidelberg for four years and graduated at Montpellier with a Doctorate in 1597.

His lecturing and teachings of the use of chemicals in medicine were not well received and were anonymously attacked, in reply to which he published a treatise in 1603 showing that the use of chemical remedies was in accord with and practised by Hippocrates and Galen. But nevertheless he was deprived of his office by the College of Physicians in Paris and ceased lecturing. However, an English peer, whom Mayerne had treated and cured, took him to England where he became physician to the Queen and later to the King. He was recognised and acknowledged by the English and his records of patients' illnesses were always minutely recorded. He treated James I on numerous occasions (mainly for gout!), and revisited France periodically. He was in turn visited by French noblemen for treatment in England, having established an international reputation. On 14 July 1624 he was knighted, and after Charles I's accession to the throne he was appointed physician to both the King and Queen.

His pharmacological experiments produced calomel and black-wash, and he did some research and development in various pigments, particularly in enamel. He even made a washable tablet-book by covering parchment with a resinous compound. In addition to a considerable interest in cooking he was granted a patent for distilling 'strong waters' and with Thomas Cadman drew up the rules of the Distillers' Company in 1638. A man of many parts . . . There is a portrait of him in the College of Physicians and a drawing by Rubens, in the British Museum.

After Charles I's execution he was appointed physician to Charles II and in the same year retired and died in Chelsea on 22 March 1655. He bequeathed his considerable library to the College of Physicians, which was unfortunately burnt in the Great Fire of 1666.

JOHN FARLEY, 1783

Biographical details of this remarkable man are not to be traced, but of the London Tavern, where he was Principal Cook, or, as we should say 'head chef', we know a little more. Some idea of this magnificent building can be gathered from the plate accompanying his portrait, and it was without question one of the city's most famous. It had been built only a few years before on the site of an older tavern, 'The White Horse', which had been gutted by fire in 1765. There is a record (1782) that the annual officers' dinners of some twenty-eight different regiments were held there; annual balls, masonic lodges, meetings, sales, charities etc, alternated with the more directly festive celebrations attending such a place. Its reputation for a fine table was a byword, and assisted Farley's successful publication for that reason. The book itself is extremely comprehensive and well-arranged, unlike most of its haphazard forerunners which often slipped in a domestic hint or two (eg 'To get rid of bed bugges') between recipes. It even included a chapter on *Elegant Ornaments for a Grand Entertainment*, which involved the sort of confectionery monstrosities popular a hundred years later, with elaborate instructions for making A floating Island, A Chinese Temple or Obelisk, A Dish of Snow, Moonshine, Solomon's Temple etc, which tend to show the type of banquet prepared under his able hand.

HANNAH GLASSE, EIGHTEENTH CENTURY

The real identity of the author of *The Art of Cooking made Plain and Easy* has remained a biographer's puzzle ever since its first appearance in 1747. She has been variously described as the wife of an attorney in Carey St, then, significantly, the name appears as a bankrupt in *The Gentleman's Magazine* for 1750, with the description: 'Warehouse-keeper of St Pauls, Covent Garden.' By 1754 the title page of the book describes the author as 'Habit Maker to Her Royal Highness the Princess of Wales'. Many years later, when the book was still selling well, the authorship was the subject of speculation in polite circles. At a dinner-party, attended by Dr Johnson and Boswell at the house of a well-known bookseller, John Dilly, the latter remarked: 'Mrs Glasse's *Cookery*, which is the best, was written by Dr Hill. Half the trade knows this.' It was just possible that Hill, if not the author, may have assisted. He was a well-known character, apothecary turned literary hack, even assaying the Drama in the course of a prodigious output. It was of him that David Garrick was moved to write a rhymed epigram:

> For physics and farces his equal there scarce is
> His farces are physics, his physics a farce is.

Whoever the author, the book certainly had a wide readership, going through fifty-two editions between 1747 and 1803, but a final edition is dated 1852. The book, rarely read today, is usually dismissed as quaint and impracticable, but I have found that with a little patience and understanding she can be tamed for occasional service in the kitchen of today. At all events she despised the French and the fashion of employing French cooks to the point where her English indignation obliged her to write the following tirade:

"A *Frenchman* in his own country will dress a fine dinner of twenty dishes, and all genteel and pretty, for the expence he will put an English lord to for priceing one lunch . . . I have heard of a cook that used six pounds of butter to fry twelve eggs; when every body knows (that understands cooking) that half a pound is full enough, or more than need be used: but then it would not be *French.* So much is the blind folly of this Age that they would rather be imposed on by a *French* booby, than give encouragement to a good *English* cook!"

SIR KENELM DIGBY, KNIGHT, 1603-65

Sir Kenelm Digby has been described by a contemporary as a handsome, witty, gay, observant, experimental, loquacious, and discursive cavalier. Hardly an intellectual, he was half-scientist and half-alchemist—'The matchless Digby, wonder of his age.' But it was his naval triumph which gave him his great reputation, and his romantic marriage endeared him to the artists of his day.

Due to his father's fatal involvement in the Gunpowder Plot, Sir Kenelm's childhood is obscure, his mother having taken him and his brother to live quietly in Buckinghamshire. There he formed a passionate attachment to Venetia, their neighbour Sir Edward Stanley's elder daughter, and when he was sent abroad to complete his education, he considered himself engaged to her.

A great traveller, in 1620 he followed the French court to Angers, where he was a popular figure, and finally fled the flagrant advances of Maria de Medici, formerly Queen Regent of France, spending the next two years in Florence.

He was summoned thence by his uncle to the Spanish court, and following an abortive effort to acquire the Infanta of Spain as a wife for Prince Charles, he returned in the Prince's retinue to England in October 1623 after three and a half years abroad. He was knighted by

James I and appointed Gentleman of the Privy Chamber to Prince Charles.

He then sought out his beloved Venetia, only to find her openly living under the protection of a married man, Sir Edward Sackville, later Earl of Dorset, and with three children! Despite this, they eventually married. Digby's position at court, however, was unaffected by the scandal and his private life continued happy. Venetia's beauty and ability to entertain led to lasting associations with such prominent men as Ben Jonson and Edward Hyde. But his financial position was at low ebb, and he decided to seek his fortune at sea, but was refused money by James I for his naval venture and so furnished two ships with the last of his resources and mounted an expedition to Scanderoon (Alexandretta) where he had several naval successes. Before his departure, Charles had acceded to the throne but his enemy Buckingham's dire influence remained, and even on his assassination there was but little improvement. Digby accordingly retired for a few years, unhonoured and unpaid for his activities on behalf of the Crown.

In 1633 Venetia died, inspiring from her many admirers a string of panegyric poems (Van Dyck had painted her several times), and her grief-stricken husband spent two years in seclusion at Gresham College.

His temporary retirement was followed by further reckless activities at home and abroad, including the killing of a French nobleman in a duel, which landed him in prison in England, his offence being that 'he had refused to pay ship money to King Charles'. An ironical accusation, since he had sunk the last of his meagre fortune into Charles's coffers in an attempt to rescue the English Court from debt. He was finally released and banished to France, but was again called upon to help the Stuart cause for Charles's wife, Henrietta Maria. Acting as ambassador, he achieved one successful mission to obtain money from the Vatican, and then retired to Calais. He returned to England only to be banished once more. At last, however, his friend John Evelyn, the diarist, obtained the permission for his return in 1651 and in 1653 he was living at Evelyn's home in Wooton.

He was in Paris in 1655 with a mission where his reputation as a scientist had been enhanced by his *Sympathetic Powder*, described in his book *On the Cure of Wounds* and probably this was the reason for his visit.

In May 1660 the restoration of the Stuarts saw his return to England. His house in Covent Garden, then the most fashionable residential district in London, was famous for its hospitality. But four years later, for some unspecified offence, he was forbidden the Court once more.

In 1665, suffering acutely from the illness then known as 'the stone', Sir Kenelm attempted a trip to Paris to see surgeons, but had to turn back, and on 11 June of that year died.

He was the author of several books of a religious and quasi-scientific character, but the most famous, quoted here, was published posthumously by his son, who delivered himself in the preface of the resounding and famous phrase in Restoration English: 'There needs no Rhetoricating Floscules to set it off.'

Glossary of Obsolete Terms

Bombard: cannon ball, and by inference a jug for liquor.

Braided: bruised.

Caudle: often a gruel, but sometimes used to mean a lear qv.

Florendine: term used indiscriminately for tart, pies etc.

Fraze (Phraise): this term is used in differing senses, mostly for dishes prepared in the frying-pan.

Lear: a thickened sauce for pies.

Mutchkin: a pint measure.

Neat: a calf or young heifer; usually applied to tongue or feet.

Pill: peel.

Rape (vinegar): grape stalks or refuse of pressed grapes used in making vinegar.

Searce: a sieve or process of sieving.

Sodde: boiled, infused.

Verjuice: acid vinegar of unripe grapes, crabapples or other sour fruit.

Acknowledgements

My particular thanks are due to all those who have allowed me access to their treasured old family manuscript books, viz: Miss M. Aldred, FRSA, Budleigh Salterton, Devon; Mrs J. Bowering, Poole, Dorset; Miss Yolande Clements, Reigate, Surrey; Mrs Phillipa Gregory, Saffron Walden, Essex; Miss M. Gwynedd Hull, Poulton-le-Fylde, Lancashire; Mrs I. Smith, Uttoxeter, Staffordshire; Mrs Rosemary Waterhouse, Windsor, Berkshire; Mrs Margaret L. Higgs, Trowbridge, Wiltshire; and J. Stevens Cox, FSA, and Mrs Cladia Roden for permission to quote their copyright material; to D. Cox Esq, Chief Librarian of the Brotherton Library in the University of Leeds, and especially for the assistance received from Mr R. Davis and Miss C. A. Wilson of the same department in examining the magnificent collection of both printed books and manuscripts totalling well over 1,500 which are substantially the gift in 1939 of Blanche Legat Leigh (Lady Mayoress in 1935–6). The university also houses another fine storehouse of culinary information in the Preston Collection of Cookery Books dating from the sixteenth century to the first edition of 'Mrs Beeton'. Other valuable assistance I acknowledge from Mr Michael Ashlin, Mr Edmund L. Childs, Mr John Moyes, Mrs Hilary Haywood, and particularly from Lin Yates (Mrs Anthony Yates) who not only researched and typed many of the receipts, but also cooked and ate them with me.

Index